perfect
muffins & bakes

This is a Parragon Publishing book
First published in 2006

Parragon Publishing
Queen Street House
4 Queen Street
Bath BA1 1HE, UK

Printed in China

This book uses imperial, metric, and US cup measurements. Follow the same units of measurement throughout; do not mix imperial and metric. All spoon measurements are level, unless otherwise stated: teaspoons are assumed to be 5ml, and tablespoons are assumed to be 15ml. Unless otherwise stated, milk is assumed to be whole, eggs and individual fruits such as bananas are medium, and pepper is freshly ground black pepper.

Recipes using raw or very lightly cooked eggs should be avoided by infants, the elderly, pregnant women, convalescents, and anyone suffering from an illness. Pregnant and breast-feeding women are advised to avoid eating peanuts and peanut products.

perfect
muffins
& bakes

introduction

Muffins, cupcakes, cookies, bars, and traybakes are without doubt the most versatile sweet treat you can make. While a large cake looks impressive, especially if it is beautifully decorated with frosting, it can really only be eaten from a plate, probably with a dessert fork. An individual cake, on the other hand, will travel, making it ideal for putting in a lunch bag, taking on a picnic, even just taken into the garden for a mid-morning or afternoon snack.

This really does not make an individual cake any less special, however, because—as you will discover when you start baking—these one-person treasures are packed full of the most sumptuous

ingredients, from fresh or dried fruits to chocolate and nuts. We've even included an equally delicious "healthy options" section so that you won't miss out if you are keeping an eye on your intake of fats and sugar.

Of course, practicality isn't always the first consideration, and there are plenty of ideas for making sweet treats with more than a hint of indulgence! Frostings, decorations, and flavorings such as liqueurs turn a cake into a celebration, and we've included a section especially for those special occasions in life. The romantic at heart can chart a whole marriage in muffins, cupcakes, and cookies, from Valentine's day and the wedding day to the baby shower and the silver and golden wedding anniversaries, with all the birthday parties and other festive occasions along the way!

Baking is a great way to pass the time on a rainy day, and these recipes are ideal for children to help with—muffins and

cupcakes need very little mixing, and take only minutes to cook. Children will love helping to decorate gingerbread people, party cookies, fairy cakes, and cupcakes to celebrate Christmas, Easter, and Halloween—and they will certainly love to eat them, too!

fruit & nut

Children can be notoriously difficult when it comes to eating fruit and vegetables, but they are soon converted when they try Apple and Cinnamon Muffins, warm from the oven and sprinkled with crushed sugar lumps, Spicy Carrot and Orange Cupcakes with Mascarpone Frosting, or Summer Fruit Tartlets, a delicious nutty pastry shell with currants and berries nestling on a cream cheese filling.

Muffins are the ideal lunch bag treat because they are relatively low in fat and sugar, and—as long as your child doesn't have a nut allergy—you can add in some useful protein. Try Banana Pecan Muffins, or Nectarine and Banana.

If you are having friends round for morning coffee or afternoon tea and want to serve something a little more sophisticated, you will really be spoilt for choice. Try Fig and Almond Muffins, or Fudge Nut Muffins—both heavenly! Warm Strawberry Cupcakes, baked in a teacup, will be a wonderful talking point and solve the mystery as to why cupcakes are so called!

If you don't mind getting sticky fingers, the Frosted Peanut Butter Cupcakes are gorgeous, and Baklava, a Middle Eastern specialty of crisp filo pastry packed with a spicy nut mixture and topped with orange-flavor syrup, is irresistibly messy to eat!

apple & cinnamon muffins

ingredients

MAKES 6

3 oz/85 g/scant $^2/_3$ cup all-purpose whole-wheat flour

$2^1/_2$ oz/70 g/$^1/_2$ cup all-purpose white flour

$1^1/_2$ tsp baking powder

pinch of salt

1 tsp ground cinnamon

$1^1/_2$ oz/40 g/scant $^1/_4$ cup golden superfine sugar

2 small eating apples, peeled, cored, and finely chopped

4 fl oz/125 ml/$^1/_2$ cup milk

1 egg, beaten

4 tbsp butter, melted

topping

12 brown sugar lumps, coarsely crushed

$^1/_2$ tsp ground cinnamon

method

1 Place 6 muffin paper liners in a muffin pan.

2 Sift both flours, baking powder, salt, and cinnamon together into a large bowl and stir in the sugar and chopped apples. Place the milk, egg, and butter in a separate bowl and mix. Add the wet ingredients to the dry ingredients and gently stir until just combined.

3 Divide the batter evenly among the paper liners. To make the topping, mix the crushed sugar lumps and cinnamon together and sprinkle over the muffins. Bake in a preheated oven, 400°F/ 200°C, for 20–25 minutes, or until risen and golden. Remove the muffins from the oven and serve warm or place them on a cooling rack and let cool.

cranberry & cheese muffins

ingredients

MAKES 18

butter, for greasing

8 oz/225 g/generous
   1^1/$_2$ cups all-purpose flour

2 tsp baking powder

^{1}/$_2$ tsp salt

2 oz/55 g/^{1}/$_4$ cup
   superfine sugar

4 tbsp butter, melted

2 large eggs, lightly beaten

6 fl oz/175 ml/^{3}/$_4$ cup milk

4 oz/115 g/generous 1 cup
   fresh cranberries

1 oz/25 g/^{1}/$_4$ cup freshly
   grated Parmesan cheese

method

1 Lightly grease 2 x 9-cup muffin pans with butter.

2 Sift the flour, baking powder, and salt into a mixing bowl. Stir in the superfine sugar.

3 In a separate bowl, combine the butter, beaten eggs, and milk, then pour into the bowl of dry ingredients. Mix lightly together until all of the ingredients are evenly combined, then stir in the fresh cranberries.

4 Divide the batter evenly among the prepared 18 cups in the muffin pans. Sprinkle the grated Parmesan cheese over the top. Transfer to a preheated oven, 400°F/200°C, and bake for 20 minutes, or until the muffins are well risen and a golden brown color.

5 Remove the muffins from the oven and let them cool slightly in the pans. Place the muffins on a cooling rack and let cool completely.

dried cherry cheesecake muffins

ingredients

MAKES 12

5½ oz/150 g butter, plus
    extra for greasing
7 oz/200 g/scant 1 cup
    cream cheese
5½ oz/150 g/generous
    ¾ cup superfine sugar
3 large eggs, lightly beaten
10½ oz/300 g/2 cups
    self-rising flour
3½ oz/100 g/generous
    ½ cup dried cherries,
    chopped
confectioners' sugar,
    for dusting

method

1 Grease a deep 12-cup muffin pan.

2 Melt the butter and let cool slightly. In a large bowl, whisk the cream cheese and sugar together, add the eggs one at a time until well combined, and then stir in the melted butter.

3 Mix the flour and cherries in a bowl, then stir gently into the batter. Spoon into the prepared muffin pan, filling each hole to about two-thirds full, and bake in a preheated oven, 350°F/180°C, for 12–15 minutes, or until golden brown. Remove from the oven and let cool on a wire rack. Eat warm or cold, dusted lightly with confectioners' sugar.

banana pecan muffins

ingredients

MAKES 8

5^1/$_2$ oz/150 g/generous 1 cup
   all-purpose flour
1^1/$_2$ tsp baking powder
pinch of salt
2^1/$_2$ oz/70 g/^{1}/$_3$ cup golden
   superfine sugar
4 oz/115 g/1 cup shelled
   pecans, coarsely chopped
2 large ripe bananas, mashed
5 tbsp milk
2 tbsp butter, melted
1 large egg, beaten
^{1}/$_2$ tsp vanilla extract

method

1 Place 8 muffin paper liners in a muffin pan. Sift the flour, baking powder, and salt into a bowl, add the sugar and pecans, and stir to combine.

2 Place the mashed bananas, milk, butter, egg, and vanilla extract in a separate bowl and mix together. Add the wet ingredients to the dry ingredients and gently stir until just combined.

3 Divide the batter evenly among the paper liners and bake in a preheated oven, 375°F/ 190°C, for 20–25 minutes until risen and golden. Remove the muffins from the oven and place them on a cooling rack and let cool.

nectarine & banana muffins

ingredients

SERVES 12

$2^1/_2$ fl oz/75 g/generous $^1/_3$ cup
    sunflower or peanut oil,
    plus extra for oiling
    (if using)

9 oz/250 g/generous
    $1^3/_4$ cups all-purpose flour

1 tsp baking soda

$^1/_4$ tsp salt

$^1/_4$ tsp allspice

$3^1/_2$ oz/100 g/$^1/_2$ cup
    superfine sugar

2 oz/55 g/$^1/_2$ cup shelled
    almonds, chopped

6 oz/175 g ripe nectarine,
    peeled and chopped

1 ripe banana, sliced

2 large eggs

3 fl oz/75 ml/$^1/_3$ cup thick
    strained plain or banana-
    flavored yogurt

1 tsp almond extract

method

1 Oil a 12-cup muffin pan with sunflower oil, or line it with 12 muffin paper liners. Sift the flour, baking soda, salt, and allspice into a mixing bowl. Then add the superfine sugar and chopped almonds and stir together.

2 In a separate large bowl, mash the nectarine and banana together, then stir in the eggs, remaining sunflower oil, yogurt, and almond extract. Add the mashed fruit mixture to the flour mixture and then gently stir together until just combined. Do not overstir the batter—it is fine for it to be a little lumpy.

3 Divide the muffin batter evenly among the 12 cups in the muffin pan or the paper liners (they should be about two-thirds full). Transfer to a preheated oven, 400°F/200°C, and bake for 20 minutes, or until risen and golden. Serve warm from the oven, or place them on a cooling rack and let cool.

tropical coconut muffins

ingredients

MAKES 12

1 tbsp sunflower or peanut
  oil, for oiling (if using)
9 oz/250 g/generous
  1¾ cups all-purpose flour
1 tsp baking powder
1 tsp baking soda
½ tsp allspice
4 oz/115 g butter
8 oz/225 g/1 cup packed
  brown sugar
2 large eggs, beaten
2 tbsp thick plain, banana, or
  pineapple-flavored yogurt
1 tbsp rum
1 ripe banana, sliced
2¾ oz/75 g canned
  pineapple rings, drained
  and chopped
⅜ cup dry unsweetened
  coconut

coconut topping

4 tbsp raw sugar
1 tsp allspice
1 oz/25 g/scant ¼ cup dry
  unsweetened coconut

method

1 Oil a 12-cup muffin pan with sunflower oil, or line it with 12 muffin paper liners. Sift the flour, baking powder, baking soda, and allspice into a mixing bowl.

2 In a separate large bowl, cream together the butter and brown sugar, then stir in the eggs, yogurt, and rum. Add the banana, pineapple, and dry unsweetened coconut and mix together gently. Add the pineapple mixture to the flour mixture and then gently stir together until just combined. Do not overstir the batter—it is fine for it to be a little lumpy.

3 Divide the muffin batter evenly among the 12 cups in the muffin pan or the paper liners (they should be about two-thirds full). To make the topping, mix the raw sugar and allspice together and sprinkle over the muffins. Sprinkle over the dry unsweetened coconut, then transfer to a preheated oven, 400°F/ 200°C. Bake for 20 minutes, or until risen and golden. Remove the muffins from the oven and serve warm, or place them on a cooling rack and let cool.

fig & almond muffins

ingredients

MAKES 12

2 tbsp sunflower or peanut
   oil, plus extra for oiling
   (if using)
9 oz/250 g/generous
   1³/₄ cups all-purpose flour
1 tsp baking soda
¹/₂ tsp salt
8 oz/225 g/1 cup raw sugar
3 oz/85 g/generous ¹/₂ cup
   dried figs, chopped
4 oz/115 g/1 cup almonds,
   chopped
7 fl oz/200 ml/1 cup water
1 tsp almond extract
2 tbsp chopped almonds,
   to decorate

method

1 Oil a 12-cup muffin pan with sunflower oil, or line it with 12 muffin paper liners. Sift the flour, baking soda, and salt into a mixing bowl. Then add the raw sugar and stir together.

2 In a separate bowl, mix the figs, almonds, and remaining sunflower oil together. Then stir in the water and almond extract. Add the fruit and nut mixture to the flour mixture and gently stir together. Do not overstir—it is fine for it to be a little lumpy.

3 Divide the muffin batter evenly among the 12 cups in the muffin pan or the paper liners (they should be about two-thirds full), then sprinkle over the remaining chopped almonds to decorate. Transfer to a preheated oven, 375°F/190°C, and bake for 25 minutes, or until risen and golden.

4 Remove the muffins from the oven and serve warm, or place them on a cooling rack and let cool.

fudge nut muffins

ingredients

MAKES 12

9 oz/250 g/generous
   1³/4 cups all-purpose flour
4 tsp baking powder
3 oz/85 g/scant ¹/2 cup
   superfine sugar
6 tbsp crunchy peanut butter
1 large egg, beaten
4 tbsp butter, melted
6 fl oz/175ml/³/4 cup milk
5¹/2 oz/150 g vanilla fudge,
   cut into small pieces
3 tbsp coarsely chopped
   unsalted peanuts

method

1 Line a 12-cup muffin pan with double muffin paper liners. Sift the flour and baking powder into a bowl. Stir in the superfine sugar. Add the peanut butter and stir until the mixture resembles bread crumbs.

2 Place the egg, butter, and milk in a separate bowl and beat until blended, then stir into the dry ingredients until just blended. Lightly stir in the fudge pieces. Divide the batter evenly among the muffin liners.

3 Sprinkle the chopped peanuts on top and bake in a preheated oven, 400°F/200°C, for 20–25 minutes until well risen and firm to the touch. Remove the muffins from the oven and let cool for 2 minutes, then place them on a cooling rack and let cool completely.

apple streusel cupcakes

ingredients

MAKES 14

$^{1}/_{2}$ tsp baking soda

10-oz/280-g jar tart applesauce

4 tbsp butter, softened,
   or soft margarine

3 oz/85 g/scant $^{1}/_{2}$ cup raw
   brown sugar

1 large egg, lightly beaten

6 oz/175 g/scant $1^{1}/_{4}$ cups
   self-rising white flour

$^{1}/_{2}$ tsp ground cinnamon

$^{1}/_{2}$ tsp freshly ground nutmeg

topping

$1^{3}/_{4}$ oz/50 g/generous $^{1}/_{3}$ cup
   all-purpose flour

$1^{3}/_{4}$ oz/50 g/$^{1}/_{4}$ cup
   raw brown sugar

$^{1}/_{4}$ tsp ground cinnamon

$^{1}/_{4}$ tsp freshly grated nutmeg

$2^{1}/_{2}$ tbsp butter

method

1 Put 14 paper baking cases in a muffin pan, or place 14 double-layer paper cases on a cookie sheet.

2 First make the topping. Put the flour, sugar, cinnamon, and nutmeg in a bowl or in the bowl of a food processor. Cut the butter into small pieces, then either rub it in by hand or blend in the processor until the mixture resembles fine bread crumbs. Set aside while you make the cakes.

3 To make the cupcakes, add the baking soda to the jar of applesauce and stir until dissolved. Put the butter and sugar in a bowl and beat together until light and fluffy. Gradually beat in the egg. Sift in the flour, cinnamon, and nutmeg and, using a large metal spoon, fold into the mixture, alternating with the applesauce.

4 Spoon the batter into the paper cases. Sprinkle the topping over each cupcake to cover the tops and press down gently.

5 Bake the cupcakes in a preheated oven, 350°F/180°C, for 20 minutes, or until well risen and golden brown. Leave the cakes for 2–3 minutes before serving warm or transfer to a wire rack and let cool.

carrot & orange cupcakes with mascarpone frosting

ingredients

MAKES 12

8 tbsp butter, softened,
    or soft margarine
4 oz/115 g/generous $1/2$ cup
    firmly packed brown sugar
juice and finely grated rind of
    1 small orange
2 large eggs, lightly beaten
6 oz/175 g carrots, grated
1 oz/25 g/$1/4$ cup walnut
    pieces, coarsely chopped
$41/2$ oz/125 g/scant 1 cup
    all-purpose flour
1 tsp ground pumpkin pie spice
$11/2$ tsp baking powder

frosting

10 oz/280 g/$11/4$ cups
    mascarpone cheese
4 tbsp confectioners' sugar
grated rind of 1 large orange

method

1 Put 12 muffin paper cases in a muffin pan.

2 Put the butter, sugar, and orange rind in a bowl and beat together until light and fluffy. Gradually add the eggs, beating well after each addition. Squeeze any excess liquid from the carrots and add to the mixture with the walnuts and orange juice. Stir into the mixture until well mixed. Sift in the flour, pumpkin pie spice, and baking powder and then, using a metal spoon, fold into the mixture. Spoon the batter into the paper cases.

3 Bake the cupcakes in a preheated oven, 350°F/180°C, for 25 minutes, or until well risen, firm to the touch, and golden brown. Transfer to a wire rack and let cool.

4 To make the frosting, put the mascarpone cheese, confectioners' sugar, and orange rind in a large bowl and beat together until well mixed.

5 When the cupcakes are cold, spread the frosting on top of each, swirling it with a round-bladed knife. Store the cupcakes in the refrigerator until ready to serve.

shredded orange cupcakes

ingredients

MAKES 12

6 tbsp butter, softened,
  or soft margarine
3 oz/85 g/scant $^1/_2$ cup
  superfine sugar
1 large egg, lightly beaten
3 oz/85 g/generous $^1/_2$ cup
  self-rising white flour
1 oz/25 g/generous $^1/_4$ cup
  ground almonds
grated rind and juice of
  1 small orange

orange topping

1 orange
2 oz/55 g/generous $^1/_4$ cup
  superfine sugar
$^1/_2$ oz/15 g/$^1/_8$ cup toasted
  slivered almonds

method

1 Put 12 paper baking cases in a muffin pan, or put 12 double-layer paper cases on a cookie sheet.

2 Put the butter and sugar in a bowl and beat together until light and fluffy. Gradually beat in the egg. Add the flour, ground almonds, and orange rind and, using a large metal spoon, fold into the mixture. Fold in the orange juice. Spoon the batter into the paper cases.

3 Bake the cupcakes in a preheated oven, 350°F/180°C, for 20–25 minutes, or until well risen and golden brown.

4 Meanwhile, make the topping. Using a citrus zester, pare the rind from the orange, then squeeze the juice. Put the rind, juice, and sugar in a pan and heat gently, stirring, until the sugar has dissolved, then let simmer for 5 minutes.

5 When the cupcakes have cooked, prick them all over with a skewer. Spoon the warm syrup and rind over each cupcake, then sprinkle the slivered almonds on top. Transfer to a wire rack and let cool.

cranberry cupcakes

ingredients

MAKES 14

5$^1/_2$ tbsp butter, softened,
   or soft margarine
3$^1/_2$ oz/100 g/$^1/_2$ cup
   superfine sugar
1 large egg
2 tbsp milk
3$^1/_2$ oz/100 g/$^3/_4$ cup
   self-rising flour
1 tsp baking powder
2$^3/_4$ oz/75 g/scant $^3/_4$ cup
   cranberries, frozen

method

1 Put 14 paper baking cases in a muffin pan, or place 14 double-layer paper cases on a cookie sheet.

2 Put the butter and sugar in a bowl and beat together until light and fluffy. Gradually beat in the egg, then stir in the milk. Sift in the flour and baking powder and, using a large metal spoon, fold them into the mixture. Gently fold in the frozen cranberries. Spoon the batter into the paper cases.

3 Bake the cupcakes in a preheated oven, 350°F/180°C, for 15–20 minutes, or until well risen and golden brown. Transfer to a wire rack and let cool.

coconut cherry cupcakes

ingredients

MAKES 12

8 tbsp butter, softened,
   or soft margarine
4 oz/115 g/generous $^{1}/_{2}$ cup
   superfine sugar
2 tbsp milk
2 eggs, lightly beaten
3 oz/85 g/generous $^{1}/_{2}$ cup
   self-rising white flour
$^{1}/_{2}$ tsp baking powder
3 oz/85 g/$^{2}/_{3}$ cup dry
   unsweetened coconut
4 oz/115 g candied
   cherries, quartered
12 whole candied,
   maraschino, or fresh
   cherries, to decorate

frosting

4 tbsp butter, softened
4 oz/115 g/1 cup
   confectioners' sugar
1 tbsp milk

method

1 Put 12 paper baking cases in a muffin pan, or place 12 double-layer paper cases on a cookie sheet.

2 Put the butter and sugar in a bowl and beat together until light and fluffy. Stir in the milk. Gradually add the eggs, beating well after each addition. Sift in the flour and baking powder and fold them in with the coconut. Gently fold in most of the quartered cherries, then spoon the batter into the paper cases and sprinkle the remaining quartered cherries over the top.

3 Bake the cupcakes in a preheated oven, 350°F/180°C, for 20–25 minutes, or until well risen, golden brown, and firm to the touch. Transfer to a wire rack and let cool.

4 To make the buttercream frosting, put the butter in a bowl and beat until fluffy. Sift in the confectioners' sugar and beat together until well mixed, gradually beating in the milk.

5 To decorate the cupcakes, using a pastry bag fitted with a large star tip, pipe the frosting on top of each cupcake, then add a candied, maraschino, or fresh cherry to decorate.

tropical pineapple cupcakes with citrus cream frosting

ingredients

MAKES 12

2 slices of canned pineapple
   in natural juice
6 tbsp butter, softened,
   or soft margarine
3 oz/85 g/scant $^1/_2$ cup
   superfine sugar
1 large egg, lightly beaten
3 oz/85 g/generous $^1/_2$ cup
   self-rising white flour
1 tbsp juice from the canned
   pineapple

frosting

2 tbsp butter, softened
3 oz/100 g/scant $^1/_2$ cup soft
   cream cheese
grated rind of 1 lemon or lime
$3^1/_2$ oz/100 g/scant 1 cup
   confectioners' sugar
1 tsp lemon juice or lime juice

method

1 Put 12 paper baking cases in a muffin pan, or place 12 double-layer paper cases on a cookie sheet.

2 Finely chop the pineapple slices. Put the butter and sugar in a bowl and beat together until light and fluffy. Gradually beat in the egg. Add the flour and, using a large metal spoon, fold into the mixture. Fold in the chopped pineapple and the pineapple juice. Spoon the batter into the paper cases.

3 Bake the cupcakes in a preheated oven, 350°F/180°C, for 20 minutes, or until well risen and golden brown. Transfer to a wire rack and let cool.

4 To make the frosting, put the butter and cream cheese in a large bowl and, using an electric hand whisk, beat together until smooth. Add the rind from the lemon or lime. Sift the confectioners' sugar into the mixture, then beat together until well mixed. Gradually beat in the juice from the lemon or lime, adding enough to form a spreading consistency.

5 When the cupcakes are cold, spread the frosting on top of each cake, or fill a pastry bag fitted with a large star tip and pipe the frosting on top. Store the cupcakes in the refrigerator until ready to serve.

warm strawberry cupcakes baked in a teacup

ingredients

MAKES 6

8 tbsp butter, softened,
plus extra for greasing

4 tbsp strawberry conserve

4 oz/115 g/generous $1/2$ cup
superfine sugar

2 eggs, lightly beaten

1 tsp vanilla extract

4 oz/115 g/generous $3/4$ cup
self-rising white flour

1 lb/450 g small whole fresh
strawberries

confectioners' sugar,
for dusting

method

1 Grease 6 heavy, round teacups with butter. Spoon 2 teaspoons of the strawberry conserve in the bottom of each teacup.

2 Put the butter and sugar in a bowl and beat together until light and fluffy. Gradually add the eggs, beating well after each addition, then add the vanilla extract. Sift in the flour and, using a large metal spoon, fold it into the mixture. Spoon the batter into the teacups.

3 Stand the cups in a roasting pan, then pour in enough hot water to come one-third up the sides of the cups. Bake the cupcakes in a preheated oven, 350ºF/180ºC, for 40 minutes, or until well risen and golden brown, and a skewer, inserted in the center, comes out clean. If over-browning, cover the cupcakes with a sheet of foil. Leave the cupcakes to cool for 2–3 minutes, then carefully lift the cups from the pan and place them on saucers.

4 Place a few of the whole strawberries on each cake, then dust them with a little sifted confectioners' sugar. Serve warm with the remaining strawberries.

moist walnut cupcakes

ingredients

MAKES 12

3 oz/85 g/^{3}/$_4$ cup walnuts
4 tbsp butter, softened
3^1/$_2$ oz/100 g/^{1}/$_2$ cup
     superfine sugar
grated rind of ^{1}/$_2$ lemon
2^1/$_2$ oz/70 g/^{1}/$_2$ cup
     self-rising white flour
2 eggs
12 walnut halves, to decorate

frosting

4 tbsp butter, softened
3 oz/85 g/^{3}/$_4$ cup
     confectioners' sugar
grated rind of ^{1}/$_2$ lemon
1 tsp lemon juice

method

1 Put 12 paper baking cases in a muffin pan, or place 12 double-layer paper cases on a cookie sheet.

2 Put the walnuts in a food processor and, using a pulsating action, blend until finely ground, being careful not to overgrind, which will turn them to oil. Add the butter, cut into small pieces, along with the sugar, lemon rind, flour, and eggs, then blend until evenly mixed. Spoon the batter into the paper cases.

3 Bake the cupcakes in a preheated oven, 375°F/190°C, for 20 minutes, or until well risen and golden brown. Transfer to a wire rack and let cool.

4 To make the frosting, put the butter in a bowl and beat until fluffy. Sift in the confectioners' sugar, add the lemon rind and juice, and mix well together.

5 When the cupcakes are cold, spread the frosting on top of each cupcake and top with a walnut half to decorate.

banana & pecan cupcakes

ingredients

MAKES 24

8 oz/225 g/generous
    1$^{1}/_{2}$ cups all-purpose flour

1$^{1}/_{4}$ tsp baking powder

$^{1}/_{4}$ tsp baking soda

2 ripe bananas

8 tbsp butter, softened,
    or soft margarine

4 oz/115 g/generous $^{1}/_{2}$ cup
    superfine sugar

$^{1}/_{2}$ tsp vanilla extract

2 eggs, lightly beaten

4 tbsp sour cream

2 oz/55 g/$^{1}/_{2}$ cup pecans,
    coarsely chopped

topping

8 tbsp butter, softened

4 oz/115 g/1 cup
    confectioners' sugar

1 oz/25 g/$^{1}/_{4}$ cup pecans,
    minced

method

1 Put 24 paper baking cases in a muffin pan, or place 24 double-layer paper cases on a cookie sheet.

2 Sift together the flour, baking powder, and baking soda. Peel the bananas; put them in a bowl, and mash with a fork.

3 Put the butter, sugar, and vanilla in a bowl and beat together until light and fluffy. Gradually add the eggs, beating well after each addition. Stir in the mashed bananas and sour cream. Using a metal spoon, fold in the sifted flour mixture and chopped nuts, then spoon the batter into the paper cases.

4 Bake the cupcakes in a preheated oven, 375°F/190°C, for 20 minutes, or until well risen and golden brown. Transfer to a wire rack and let cool.

5 To make the topping, beat the butter in a bowl until fluffy. Sift in the confectioners' sugar and mix together well. Spread the frosting on top of each cupcake and sprinkle with the minced pecans before serving.

frosted peanut butter cupcakes

ingredients

MAKES 16

4 tbsp butter, softened,
   or soft margarine
8 oz/225 g/scant 1^1/4 cups
   firmly packed brown sugar
4 oz/115 g/generous ^{1}/3 cup
   crunchy peanut butter
2 eggs, lightly beaten
1 tsp vanilla extract
8 oz/225 g/generous
   1^1/2 cups all-purpose flour
2 tsp baking powder
3^1/2 fl oz/100 ml/generous
   ^{1}/3 cup milk

frosting

7 oz/200 g/scant 1 cup
   full-fat soft cream cheese
2 tbsp butter, softened
8 oz/225 g/2 cups
   confectioners' sugar

method

1 Put 16 muffin paper cases in a muffin pan.

2 Put the butter, sugar, and peanut butter in a bowl and beat together for 1–2 minutes, or until well mixed. Gradually add the eggs, beating well after each addition, then add the vanilla extract. Sift in the flour and baking powder and then, using a metal spoon, fold them into the mixture, alternating with the milk. Spoon the batter into the paper cases.

3 Bake the cupcakes in a preheated oven, 350°F/180°C, for 25 minutes, or until well risen and golden brown. Transfer to a wire rack and let cool.

4 To make the frosting, put the cream cheese and butter in a large bowl and, using an electric hand whisk, beat together until smooth. Sift the confectioners' sugar into the mixture, then beat together until well mixed.

5 When the cupcakes are cold, spread the frosting on top of each cupcake, swirling it with a round-bladed knife. Store the cupcakes in the refrigerator until ready to serve.

maple pecan tarts

ingredients

MAKES 12

dough

5 oz/150 g/1 cup all-purpose
  flour, plus extra for dusting
6 tbsp butter
2 oz/55 g/$\frac{1}{4}$ cup golden
  superfine sugar
2 egg yolks

filling

2 tbsp maple syrup
5 fl oz/150 ml/$\frac{2}{3}$ cup
  heavy cream
4 oz/115 g/generous $\frac{1}{2}$ cup
  golden superfine sugar
pinch of cream of tartar
6 tbsp water
6 oz/185 g/1 cup pecans
12 pecan nut halves,
  to decorate

method

1 Sift the flour into a large bowl, then cut the butter into pieces and rub it into the flour using your fingertips until the mixture resembles bread crumbs. Stir in the sugar, then stir in the egg yolks to make a smooth dough. Wrap in plastic wrap and chill in the refrigerator for 30 minutes.

2 On a floured counter, roll out the pastry thinly, cut out circles, and use to line 12 tartlet pans. Prick the bottoms and press a piece of foil into each tart shell. Bake in a preheated oven, 400°F/200°C, for 10–15 minutes, or until light golden. Remove the foil and bake for a further 2–3 minutes. Let cool on a wire rack.

3 To make the filling, mix together half the maple syrup and half the cream in a bowl. Place the sugar, cream of tartar, and water in a pan over low heat and stir until the sugar dissolves. Bring to a boil and continue boiling until light golden. Remove from the heat and stir in the maple syrup and cream mixture.

4 Return to the heat and cook to the "soft ball" stage (240°F/116°C), when a little of the mixture forms a soft ball when dropped into cold water. Stir in the remaining cream and let stand until warm. Brush the remaining syrup over the edges of the tarts. Place the pecans in the shells, spoon in the toffee and top with a nut half. Let cool.

baklava

ingredients

MAKES 20 PIECES

4 oz/115 g/generous $^2/_3$ cup
   blanched almonds
4 oz/115 g/generous 1 cup
   walnuts
4 oz/115 g/$^1/_2$ cup
   shelled pistachios
2 oz/55 g/$^1/_4$ cup brown sugar
1 tsp ground cinnamon
$^1/_2$ tsp freshly grated nutmeg
2 oz/55 g butter, melted, plus
   extra for greasing
12 sheets ready-made filo
   pastry, about 12 x 7 inches/
   30 x 18 cm

syrup

generous 1 cup
   granulated sugar
5 fl oz/150 ml/$^2/_3$ cup water
1 tbsp lemon juice
1 tbsp orange-flower water

method

1 To make the syrup, place the sugar, water, and lemon juice in a pan over low heat and stir until the sugar has completely dissolved, then boil gently for 5 minutes, until the mixture takes on a syrupy consistency. Add the orange-flower water and boil for an additional 2 minutes. Let cool completely.

2 Place one-third of all the nuts in a food processor and process until finely chopped. Coarsely chop the remainder. Place all the chopped nuts in a bowl with the sugar, cinnamon, and nutmeg and mix together.

3 Grease a baking pan that is roughly the same size as, or slightly smaller than, the sheets of pastry. Brush 1 sheet of pastry with butter and place on the bottom of the baking pan. Repeat with 3 more sheets. Spread one-third of the nut mixture over the pastry. Top with 2 more layers of buttered pastry, then another third of the nut mixture. Top with 2 more buttered filo sheets, then the remaining nuts. Finally top with 4 sheets of buttered filo.

4 Cut the top layer of pastry into diamonds and bake in a preheated oven, 350°F/180°C, for 30–40 minutes, or until crisp and golden. Remove from the oven, pour the syrup over the top, and cool. When cold, trim the edges and cut into diamond shapes.

summer fruit tartlets

ingredients

MAKES 12

dough

7 oz/200 g/scant 1¹/₂ cups
   all-purpose flour, plus
   extra for dusting
3 oz/85 g/generous ³/₄ cup
   confectioners' sugar
2 oz/55 g/²/₃ cup
   ground almonds
4 oz/115 g butter
1 egg yolk
1 tbsp milk

filling

8 oz/225 g/1 cup
   cream cheese
confectioners' sugar, to taste,
   plus extra for dusting
12 oz/350 g/2¹/₂ cups fresh
   summer fruits, such as
   red and white currants,
   blueberries, raspberries,
   and small strawberries

method

1 To make the dough, sift the flour and confectioners' sugar into a bowl. Stir in the ground almonds. Add the butter and rub in until the mixture resembles bread crumbs. Add the egg yolk and milk and work in with a spatula, then mix with your fingers until the dough binds together. Wrap the dough in plastic wrap and let chill in the refrigerator for 30 minutes.

2 On a floured counter, roll out the dough and use to line 12 deep tartlet or individual brioche pans. Prick the bottoms. Press a piece of foil into each tartlet, covering the edges, and bake in a preheated oven, 400°F/200°C, for 10–15 minutes, or until light golden brown. Remove the foil and bake for an additional 2–3 minutes. Transfer to a wire rack to cool.

3 To make the filling, place the cream cheese and confectioners' sugar in a bowl and mix together. Place a spoonful of filling in each tart shell and arrange the fruit on top. Dust with sifted confectioners' sugar and serve.

apple shortcakes

ingredients

MAKES 4

2 tbsp butter, cut into
   small pieces, plus extra
   for greasing
5^1/$_2$ oz/150 g/generous 1 cup
   all-purpose flour, plus
   extra for dusting
^{1}/$_2$ tsp salt
1 tsp baking powder
1 tbsp superfine sugar
2 fl oz/50 ml/^{1}/$_4$ cup milk
confectioners' sugar,
   for dusting

filling

3 dessert apples, peeled,
   cored, and sliced
3^1/$_2$ oz/100 g/^{1}/$_2$ cup
   superfine sugar
1 tbsp lemon juice
1 tsp ground cinnamon
10 fl oz/300 ml/1^1/$_4$ cups
   water
5 fl oz/150 ml/^{2}/$_3$ cup heavy
   cream, lightly whipped

method

1 Lightly grease a cookie sheet. Sift the flour, salt, and baking powder into a large bowl. Stir in the sugar, then add the butter and rub it in with your fingertips until the mixture resembles fine bread crumbs. Pour in the milk and mix to a soft dough.

2 On a lightly floured counter, knead the dough lightly, then roll out to ^{1}/2-inch/1-cm thick. Stamp out 4 circles, using a 2-inch/ 5-cm cutter. Transfer the circles to the prepared cookie sheet.

3 Bake in a preheated oven, 425°F/220°C, for 15 minutes, until the shortcakes are well risen and lightly browned. Let cool.

4 To make the filling, place the apple, sugar, lemon juice, and cinnamon in a pan. Add the water, bring to a boil and let simmer, uncovered, for 5–10 minutes, or until the apples are tender. Cool slightly, then remove the apples from the pan.

5 To serve, split the shortcakes in half. Place each bottom half on an individual serving plate and spoon on a fourth of the apple slices, then the cream. Place the other half of the shortcake on top. Serve dusted with confectioners' sugar.

raspberry éclairs

ingredients

MAKES 8

choux pastry

2 oz/55 g butter

5 fl oz/150 ml/²/₃ cup water

2¹/₂ oz/70 g/¹/₂ cup all-
  purpose flour, sifted

2 eggs, beaten

filling

11 fl oz/325 ml/1¹/₃ cups
  heavy cream

1 tbsp confectioners' sugar

6 oz/175 g/³/₄ cup fresh
  raspberries

frosting

4 oz/115 g/generous 1 cup
  confectioners' sugar

2 tsp lemon juice

pink food coloring (optional)

method

1 To make the choux pastry, place the butter and water in a large, heavy-bottom pan and bring to a boil. Add the flour, all at once, and beat thoroughly until the mixture leaves the sides of the pan. Let cool slightly, then vigorously beat in the eggs, 1 at a time.

2 Spoon the mixture into a pastry bag fitted with a ¹/₂-inch/1-cm nozzle and make 8 x 3-inch/7.5-cm lengths on several dampened cookie sheets. Bake in a preheated oven, 400°F/200°C, for 30 minutes, or until crisp and golden. Remove from the oven and make a small hole in each éclair with the tip of a knife to let out the steam, then return to the oven for an additional 5 minutes, to dry out the insides. Transfer to a wire rack to cool.

3 To make the filling, place the cream and confectioners' sugar in a bowl and whisk until thick. Split the éclairs and fill with the cream and raspberries. To make the frosting, sift the confectioners' sugar into a bowl and stir in the lemon juice and enough water to make a smooth paste. Add pink food coloring, if desired. Drizzle the frosting generously over the éclairs, and let set before serving.

cherry & sultana rockies

ingredients

MAKES 10

9 oz/250 g/1³/4 cups
   self-rising flour
1 tsp ground allspice
6 tbsp butter, plus extra
   for greasing
3 oz/85 g/scant 1¹/2 cups
   golden superfine sugar
2 oz/55 g/¹/4 cup candied
   cherries, quartered
2 oz/55 g/¹/3 cup golden
   raisins
1 egg
2 tbsp milk
raw brown sugar, for sprinkling

method

1 Sift the flour and allspice into a bowl. Add the butter and rub it in until the mixture resembles bread crumbs. Stir in the sugar, cherries, and golden raisins.

2 Break the egg into a bowl and whisk in the milk. Pour most of the egg mixture into the dry ingredients and mix with a fork to make a stiff, coarse dough, adding the rest of the egg and milk, if necessary.

3 Using 2 forks, pile the mixture into 10 rocky heaps on a greased cookie sheet. Sprinkle with raw brown sugar. Bake in a preheated oven, 400°F/200°C, for 10–15 minutes, or until golden and firm to the touch. Let cool on the cookie sheet for 2 minutes, then transfer to a wire rack to cool completely.

walnut & cinnamon blondies

ingredients

MAKES 9

4 oz/115 g butter, plus extra
   for greasing
8 oz/225 g/generous 1 cup
   brown sugar
1 egg
1 egg yolk
5 oz/150 g/1 cup
   self-rising flour
1 tsp ground cinnamon
3 oz/85 g/generous ¹/₂ cup
   coarsely chopped walnuts

method

1 Place the butter and sugar in a pan over low heat and stir until the sugar has dissolved. Cook, stirring, for an additional 1 minute. The mixture will bubble slightly, but do not let it boil. Let cool for 10 minutes.

2 Stir the egg and egg yolk into the mixture. Sift in the flour and cinnamon, add the nuts, and stir until just blended. Pour the cake batter into a greased and base-lined 7-inch/ 18-cm square cake pan, then bake in a preheated oven, 350°F/180°C, for 20–25 minutes, or until springy in the center and a skewer inserted into the center of the cake comes out clean.

3 Let cool in the pan for a few minutes, then run a knife round the edge of the cake to loosen it. Turn the cake out onto a wire rack and peel off the paper. Let cool completely. When cold, cut into squares.

chocolate

Chocolate is always a favorite ingredient in sweet treats, and so we've included a whole chapter especially for all you chocoholics! Your only problem will be where to begin!

Chocolate muffins go beautifully with coffee, so these are a great choice for your mid-morning break—there are four recipes to choose from, each with a special twist of its own. Mocha Cupcakes with Whipped Cream, Mocha Brownies—served either plain or with sour cream frosting—and Cappuccino Squares will also fit the bill to perfection, or perhaps a crisp Viennese Finger or a Double Chocolate Chip Cookie or two.

For afternoon tea, go for the Caramel Chocolate Shortbread, which is sometimes called "millionaire's shortbread." Try it, and you'll find out why! Chocolate Butterfly Cakes are also perfect at teatime, or Tiny Chocolate Cupcakes with Ganache Frosting.

If you want a little treat in the evening, the Devil's Food Cakes with Chocolate Frosting, the Warm Molten-centered Chocolate Cupcakes, and the Chocolate Tarts—made with either semisweet or white chocolate—are just out of this world. At Christmas, try Panforte di Sienna, a specialty from Tuscany in Italy—it's wonderful served with a glass of dessert wine to end a festive dinner.

spiced chocolate muffins

ingredients

MAKES 12

3½ oz/100 g butter, softened

5 oz/150 g/scant ¾ cup
   superfine sugar

4 oz/115 g/½ cup packed
   brown sugar

2 large eggs

5 fl oz/150 ml/⅔ cup
   sour cream

5 tbsp milk

9 oz/250 g/generous
   1¾ cups all-purpose flour

1 tsp baking soda

2 tbsp unsweetened cocoa

1 tsp allspice

7 oz/200 g/generous 1 cup
   semisweet chocolate chips

method

1 Line a 12-cup muffin pan with muffin liners.

2 Place the butter, superfine sugar, and brown sugar in a bowl and beat well. Beat in the eggs, sour cream, and milk until thoroughly mixed. Sift the flour, baking soda, cocoa, and allspice into a separate bowl and stir into the mixture. Add the chocolate chips and mix well. Divide the batter evenly among the paper liners. Bake in a preheated oven, 375°F/190°C, for 25–30 minutes.

3 Remove from the oven and let cool for 10 minutes. Place them on a cooling rack and let cool completely. Store in an airtight container until required.

double chocolate muffins

ingredients

MAKES 12

7 oz/200 g/scant 1^1/2 cups
   all-purpose flour
1 oz/25 g/^{1}/3 cup
   unsweetened cocoa, plus
   extra for dusting
1 tbsp baking powder
1 tsp ground cinnamon
4 oz/115 g/generous ^{1}/2 cup
   golden superfine sugar
6^1/2 oz/185 g white chocolate,
   broken into pieces
2 large eggs
3^1/2 fl oz/100 ml/generous
   ^{1}/3 cup sunflower
   or peanut oil
7 fl oz/200 ml/1 cup milk

method

1 Line a 12-cup muffin pan with muffin liners.

2 Sift the flour, cocoa, baking powder, and cinnamon into a large mixing bowl. Stir in the sugar and 4^1/2 oz/125 g of the white chocolate.

3 Place the eggs and oil in a separate bowl and whisk until frothy, then gradually whisk in the milk. Stir into the dry ingredients until just blended. Divide the batter evenly among the paper liners, filling each three-quarters full. Bake in a preheated oven, 400°F/200°C, for 20 minutes, or until well risen and springy to the touch. Remove the muffins from the oven, let cool in the pan for 2 minutes, then remove them and place them on a cooling rack to cool completely.

4 Place the remaining white chocolate in a heatproof bowl, set the bowl over a pan of barely simmering water, and heat until melted. Spread over the top of the muffins. Let set, then dust the tops with a little cocoa and serve.

chocolate chip muffins

ingredients

MAKES 12

3 tbsp soft margarine

7 oz/200 g/1 cup
 superfine sugar

2 large eggs

5 fl oz/150 ml/²/₃ cup
 whole plain yogurt

5 tbsp milk

10 oz/300 g/2 cups
 all-purpose flour

1 tsp baking soda

4 oz/115 g/1 cup semisweet
 chocolate chips

method

1 Line a 12-cup muffin pan with muffin liners.

2 Place the margarine and sugar in a mixing bowl and beat with a wooden spoon until light and fluffy. Beat in the eggs, yogurt, and milk until combined.

3 Sift the flour and baking soda into the batter. Stir until just blended.

4 Stir in the chocolate chips, then divide the batter evenly among the paper liners and bake in a preheated oven, 400°F/200°C, for 25 minutes, or until risen and golden. Remove the muffins from the oven and let cool in the pan for 5 minutes, then place them on a cooling rack to cool completely.

chocolate orange muffins

ingredients

MAKES 9

sunflower or peanut oil,
  for oiling

5 oz/150 g/scant 1 cup
  self-rising white flour

5 oz/150 g/scant 1 cup self-
  rising whole-wheat flour

2 oz/55 g/generous $^{1}/_{4}$ cup
  ground almonds

2 oz/55 g/generous $^{1}/_{4}$ cup
  packed brown sugar

rind and juice of 1 orange

6 oz/175 g/$^{3}/_{4}$ cup
  cream cheese

2 large eggs

2 oz/55 g/$^{1}/_{3}$ cup semisweet
  chocolate chips

method

1 Thoroughly oil a 9-cup muffin pan.

2 Sift both flours into a mixing bowl and stir in the ground almonds and sugar.

3 Mix the orange rind and juice, cream cheese, and eggs together in a separate bowl. Make a well in the center of the dry ingredients and stir in the wet ingredients, then add the chocolate chips. Beat well to combine all the ingredients.

4 Divide the batter among the cups, filling each no more than three-quarters full. Bake in a preheated oven, 375°F/190°C, for 20–25 minutes until well risen and golden brown.

5 Remove the muffins from the oven and let cool slightly on a cooling rack, but eat them as fresh as possible.

dark & white fudge cupcakes

ingredients

MAKES 20

7 fl oz/100 ml/scant
    1 cup water
6 tbsp butter
3 oz/85 g/scant $^1/_2$ cup
    superfine sugar
1 tbsp corn syrup
3 tbsp milk
1 tsp vanilla extract
1 tsp baking soda
8 oz/225 g/generous
    1$^1/_2$ cups all-purpose flour
2 tbsp unsweetened cocoa

topping

1$^3/_4$ oz/50 g semisweet
    chocolate
4 tbsp water
3$^1/_2$ tbsp butter
1$^3/_4$ oz/50 g white chocolate
12 oz/350 g/3 cups
    confectioners' sugar

chocolate curls

3$^1/_2$ oz/100 g semisweet
    chocolate
3$^1/_2$ oz/100 g white chocolate

method

1 Put 20 paper baking cases in 2 muffin pans, or place 20 double-layer paper cases on 2 baking sheets.

2 Put the water, butter, superfine sugar, and syrup in a pan. Heat gently, stirring, until the sugar has dissolved, then bring to a boil. Reduce the heat and cook gently for 5 minutes. Remove from the heat and let cool.

3 Meanwhile, put the milk and vanilla extract in a bowl. Add the baking soda and stir to dissolve. Sift the flour and cocoa into a separate bowl and add the syrup mixture. Stir in the milk and beat until smooth. Spoon the batter into the paper cases until they are two-thirds full. Bake the cupcakes in a preheated oven, 350°F/180°C, for 20 minutes, or until well risen and firm to the touch. Transfer to a wire rack and let cool.

4 To make the topping, break the semisweet chocolate into a small heatproof bowl, add half the water and half the butter, and melt over a pan of gently simmering water. Stir until smooth and let stand over the water. Using another bowl, repeat with the white chocolate and remaining water and butter. Sift half the sugar into each bowl and beat until smooth and thick. Top the cupcakes with the frostings and let set. Decorate with chocolate curls made by shaving the chocolate with a potato peeler.

warm molten-centered chocolate cupcakes

ingredients

MAKES 8

4 tbsp soft margarine

2 oz/55 g/generous $1/4$ cup
    superfine sugar

1 large egg

3 oz/85 g/generous $1/2$ cup
    self-rising flour

1 tbsp unsweetened cocoa

2 oz/55 g semisweet
    chocolate

confectioners' sugar,
    for dusting

method

1 Put 8 paper baking cases in a muffin pan, or place 8 double-layer paper cases on a cookie sheet.

2 Put the margarine, sugar, egg, flour, and cocoa in a large bowl and, using an electric hand whisk, beat together until just smooth.

3 Spoon half of the batter into the paper cases. Using a teaspoon, make an indentation in the center of each cake. Break the chocolate evenly into 8 squares and place a piece in each indentation, then spoon the remaining cake batter on top.

4 Bake the cupcakes in a preheated oven, 375°F/190°C, for 20 minutes, or until well risen and springy to the touch. Leave the cupcakes for 2–3 minutes before serving warm, dusted with sifted confectioners' sugar.

jumbo chocolate chip cupcakes

ingredients

MAKES 8

7 tbsp soft margarine

$3^1/_2$ oz/100 g/$^1/_2$ cup
superfine sugar

2 large eggs

$3^1/_2$ oz/100 g/scant $^3/_4$ cup
self-rising white flour

$3^1/_2$ oz/100 g/generous
$^1/_2$ cup semisweet
chocolate chips

method

1 Put 8 muffin paper cases in a muffin pan.

2 Put the margarine, sugar, eggs, and flour in a large bowl and, using an electric hand whisk, beat together until just smooth. Fold in the chocolate chips. Spoon the batter into the paper cases.

3 Bake the cupcakes in a preheated oven, 375°F/190°C, for 20–25 minutes, or until well risen and golden brown. Transfer to a wire rack to cool.

mocha cupcakes with whipped cream

ingredients

MAKES 20

2 tbsp instant espresso
  coffee powder
6 tbsp butter
3 oz/85 g/scant $^1/_2$ cup
  superfine sugar
1 tbsp honey
7 fl oz/200 ml/scant 1 cup
  water
8 oz/225 g/generous
  $1^1/_2$ cups all-purpose flour
2 tbsp unsweetened cocoa
1 tsp baking soda
3 tbsp milk
1 large egg, lightly beaten

topping

8 fl oz/225 ml/1 cup
  whipping cream
unsweetened cocoa, sifted,
  for dusting

method

1 Put 20 paper baking cases in 2 muffin pans, or place 20 double-layer paper cases on 2 baking sheets.

2 Put the coffee powder, butter, sugar, honey, and water in a pan and heat gently, stirring, until the sugar has dissolved. Bring to a boil, then reduce the heat and let simmer for 5 minutes. Pour into a large heatproof bowl and let cool.

3 When the mixture has cooled, sift in the flour and cocoa. Dissolve the baking soda in the milk, then add to the mixture with the egg and beat together until smooth. Spoon the batter into the paper cases.

4 Bake the cupcakes in a preheated oven, 350°F/180°C, for 15–20 minutes, or until well risen and firm to the touch. Transfer to a wire rack to cool.

5 For the topping, whisk the cream in a bowl until it holds its shape. Just before serving, spoon heaped teaspoonfuls of cream on top of each cake, then dust lightly with sifted cocoa. Store the cupcakes in the refrigerator until ready to serve.

chocolate cupcakes with cream cheese frosting

ingredients

MAKES 18

6 tbsp butter, softened,
   or soft margarine
3^1/$_2$ oz/100 g/^{1}/$_2$ cup
   superfine sugar
2 eggs, lightly beaten
2 tbsp milk
2 oz/55 g/^{1}/$_3$ cup semisweet
   chocolate chips
8 oz/225 g/generous 1^1/$_2$
   cups self-rising white flour
1 oz/25 g/generous ^{1}/$_4$ cup
   unsweetened cocoa

frosting

8 oz/225 g white chocolate
5^1/$_2$ oz/150 g/generous
   ^{2}/$_3$ cup lowfat
   cream cheese

method

1 Put 18 paper baking cases in 2 muffin pans, or place 18 double-layer paper cases on a cookie sheet.

2 Put the butter and sugar in a bowl and beat together until light and fluffy. Gradually add the eggs, beating well after each addition. Add the milk, then fold in the chocolate chips. Sift in the flour and cocoa, then fold into the mixture. Spoon the batter into the paper cases and smooth the tops.

3 Bake the cupcakes in a preheated oven, 400°F/200°C, for 20 minutes, or until well risen and springy to the touch. Transfer to a wire rack and let cool.

4 To make the frosting, break the chocolate into a small heatproof bowl and set the bowl over a pan of gently simmering water until melted. Let cool slightly. Put the cream cheese in a bowl and beat until softened, then beat in the slightly cooled chocolate.

5 Spread a little of the frosting over the top of each cupcake, then let chill in the refrigerator for 1 hour before serving.

tiny chocolate cupcakes with ganache frosting

ingredients

MAKES 20

4 tbsp butter, softened

2 oz/55 g/generous ¼ cup
   superfine sugar

1 large egg, lightly beaten

2 oz/55 g/scant ½ cup white
   self-rising flour

2 tbsp unsweetened cocoa

1 tbsp milk

20 chocolate-coated coffee
   beans, to decorate
   (optional)

frosting

3½ oz/100 g semisweet
   chocolate

3½ fl oz/100 ml/generous
   ⅓ cup heavy cream

method

1 Put 20 double-layer mini paper cases on 2 baking sheets.

2 Put the butter and sugar in a bowl and beat together until light and fluffy. Gradually beat in the egg. Sift in the flour and cocoa and then, using a metal spoon, fold them into the mixture. Stir in the milk.

3 Fill a pastry bag, fitted with a large plain tip, with the batter and pipe it into the paper cases, filling each one until half full.

4 Bake the cakes in a preheated oven, 375°F/ 190°C, for 10–15 minutes, or until well risen and firm to the touch. Transfer to a wire rack to cool.

5 To make the frosting, break the chocolate into a pan and add the cream. Heat gently, stirring all the time, until the chocolate has melted. Pour into a large heatproof bowl and, using an electric hand whisk, beat the mixture for 10 minutes, or until thick, glossy and cool.

6 Fill a pastry bag, fitted with a large star tip, with the frosting and pipe a swirl on top of each cupcake. Alternatively, spoon over the frosting. Chill in the refrigerator for 1 hour before serving. Serve decorated with a chocolate-coated coffee bean, if liked.

devil's food cakes with chocolate frosting

ingredients

MAKES 18

3^1/$_2$ tbsp soft margarine

4 oz/115 g/generous ^{1}/$_2$ cup firmly packed brown sugar

2 large eggs

4 oz/115 g/generous ^{3}/$_4$ cup all-purpose flour

^{1}/$_2$ tsp baking soda

1 oz/25 g/generous ^{1}/$_4$ cup unsweetened cocoa

4 fl oz/125 ml/^{1}/$_2$ cup sour cream

frosting

4^1/$_2$ oz/125 g semisweet chocolate

2 tbsp superfine sugar

5 fl oz/150 ml/^{2}/$_3$ cup sour cream

chocolate curls

(optional)

3^1/$_2$ oz/100 g semisweet chocolate

method

1 Put 18 paper baking cases in a muffin pan, or put 18 double-layer paper cases on a cookie sheet.

2 Put the margarine, sugar, eggs, flour, baking soda, and cocoa in a large bowl and, using an electric hand whisk, beat together until just smooth. Using a metal spoon, fold in the sour cream. Spoon the batter into the paper cases.

3 Bake the cupcakes in a preheated oven, 350°F/180°C, for 20 minutes, or until well risen and firm to the touch. Transfer to a wire rack to cool.

4 To make the frosting, break the chocolate into a heatproof bowl. Set the bowl over a pan of gently simmering water and heat until melted, stirring occasionally. Remove from the heat and let cool slightly, then whisk in the sugar and sour cream until combined. Spread the frosting over the tops of the cupcakes and let set in the refrigerator before serving. If liked, serve decorated with chocolate curls made by shaving semisweet chocolate with a potato peeler.

chocolate butterfly cakes

ingredients

MAKES 12

8 tbsp soft margarine

3¹/₂ oz/100 g/¹/₂ cup
   superfine sugar

5¹/₂ oz/150 g/generous
   1¹/₂ cups self-rising
   white flour

2 large eggs

2 tbsp unsweetened cocoa

1 oz/25 g semisweet
   chocolate, melted

confectioners' sugar,
   for dusting

filling

6 tbsp butter, softened

6 oz/175 g/1¹/₂ cups
   confectioners' sugar

1 oz/25 g semisweet
   chocolate, melted

method

1 Put 12 paper baking cases in a muffin pan, or put 12 double-layer paper cases on a cookie sheet.

2 Put the margarine, sugar, flour, eggs, and cocoa in a large bowl and, using an electric hand whisk, beat together until just smooth. Beat in the melted chocolate. Spoon the batter into the paper cases, filling them three-fourths full.

3 Bake the cupcakes in a preheated oven, 350°F/180°C, for 15 minutes, or until springy to the touch. Transfer to a wire rack and let cool completely.

4 To make the filling, put the butter in a bowl and beat until fluffy. Sift in the confectioners' sugar and beat together until smooth. Add the melted chocolate and beat until well mixed.

5 When the cupcakes are cold, use a serrated knife to cut a circle from the top of each cake and then cut each circle in half. Spread or pipe a little of the buttercream into the center of each cupcake and press the 2 semicircular halves into it at an angle to resemble butterfly wings. Dust with sifted confectioners' sugar before serving.

mocha brownies

ingredients

MAKES 16

2 oz/55 g butter, plus extra
for greasing

4 oz/115 g semisweet
chocolate, broken into
pieces

6 oz/175 g/scant 1 cup
brown sugar

2 eggs

1 tbsp instant coffee powder,
dissolved in 1 tbsp hot
water, cooled

3 oz/85 g/scant $^2/_3$ cup
all-purpose flour

$^1/_2$ tsp baking powder

2 oz/55 g/$^1/_3$ cup coarsely
chopped pecans

method

1 Grease and line the bottom of an 8-inch/
20-cm square cake pan. Place the butter and
chocolate in a heavy-bottom pan over low heat
until melted. Stir and let cool.

2 Place the sugar and eggs in a large bowl and
cream together until light and fluffy. Fold in
the chocolate mixture and cooled coffee and
mix thoroughly. Sift in the flour and baking
powder and lightly fold into the mixture, then
carefully fold in the pecans.

3 Pour the batter into the prepared pan and
bake in a preheated oven, 350°F/180°C, for
25–30 minutes, or until firm and a skewer
inserted into the center comes out clean.

4 Let cool in the pan for a few minutes, then
run a knife round the edge of the cake to
loosen it. Turn the cake out onto a wire rack
and peel off the lining paper. Let cool
completely. When cold, cut into squares.

mocha brownies with sour cream frosting

ingredients

**MAKES 9 LARGE OR
16 SMALL BROWNIES**

2 oz/55 g butter, plus extra
   for greasing
4 oz/115 g semisweet
   chocolate, broken
   into pieces
6 oz/175 g/$^3/_4$ cup
   dark brown sugar
2 eggs
2 tbsp strong coffee, cooled
3 oz/85 g/generous $^1/_2$ cup
   all-purpose flour
$^1/_2$ tsp baking powder
pinch of salt
2 oz/55 g/$^1/_4$ cup shelled
   walnuts, chopped

frosting

4 oz/115 g semisweet
   chocolate, broken
   into pieces
5 fl oz/150 ml/$^2/_3$ cup
   sour cream

method

1 Place the butter and chocolate in a small heatproof bowl and set over a pan of gently simmering water until melted. Stir until smooth. Remove from the heat and let cool.

2 Beat the sugar and eggs together until pale and thick. Fold in the chocolate mixture and coffee. Mix well. Sift the flour, baking powder, and salt into the cake batter and fold in. Fold in the walnuts. Pour the cake batter into a greased 8-inch/20-cm square cake pan base-lined with parchment paper and bake in a preheated oven, 350°F/180°C, for 20–25 minutes, or until set. Let cool in the pan.

3 To make the frosting, melt the chocolate. Stir in the sour cream and beat until evenly blended. Spoon the topping over the brownies and make a swirling pattern with a spatula. Let set in a cool place. Cut into squares, then remove from the pan and serve.

cappuccino squares

ingredients

MAKES 15

8 oz/225 g butter, softened,
plus extra for greasing

8 oz/225 g/generous
1½ cups self-rising flour

1 tsp baking powder

1 tsp unsweetened cocoa,
plus extra for dusting

8 oz/225 g/generous 1 cup
golden superfine sugar

4 eggs, beaten

3 tbsp instant coffee powder,
dissolved in 2 tbsp hot water

white chocolate frosting

4 oz/115 g white chocolate,
broken into pieces

2 oz/55 g butter, softened

3 tbsp milk

6 oz/175 g/1¾ cups
confectioners' sugar

method

1 Grease and line the bottom of a shallow 11 x 7-inch/28 x 18-cm pan. Sift the flour, baking powder, and cocoa into a bowl and add the butter, superfine sugar, eggs, and coffee. Beat well, by hand or with an electric whisk, until smooth, then spoon into the pan and smooth the top.

2 Bake in a preheated oven, 350°F/180°C, for 35–40 minutes, or until risen and firm. Let cool in the pan for 10 minutes, then turn out onto a wire rack and peel off the lining paper. Let cool completely. To make the frosting, place the chocolate, butter, and milk in a bowl set over a pan of simmering water and stir until the chocolate has melted.

3 Remove the bowl from the pan and sift in the confectioners' sugar. Beat until smooth, then spread over the cake. Dust the top of the cake with sifted cocoa, then cut into squares.

panforte di siena

ingredients

SERVES 12–16

butter, for greasing

2 oz/55 g/¼ cup candied
   cherries, quartered

4 oz/115 g/²/₃ cup mixed
   candied orange and lemon
   peel, finely chopped

2 tbsp candied ginger,
   coarsely chopped

4 oz/115 g/1 cup
   slivered almonds

4 oz/115 g/³/₄ cup hazelnuts,
   toasted and
   coarsely ground

2 oz/55 g/scant ½ cup
   all-purpose flour

1 oz/25 g/¼ cup
   unsweetened cocoa

1 tsp ground cinnamon

¼ tsp ground cloves

¼ tsp ground nutmeg

¼ tsp ground coriander

4 oz/115 g/¹/₃ cup honey

4 oz/115 g/generous ½ cup
   golden superfine sugar

1 tsp orange flower water

confectioners' sugar,
   for dusting

method

1 Thoroughly grease the bottom of an 8-inch/20-cm loose-bottom cake or tart pan. Line the bottom with nonstick parchment paper. Place the cherries, candied peel, ginger, almonds, and hazelnuts in a bowl. Sift in the flour, cocoa, cinnamon, cloves, nutmeg, and coriander, and mix. Set aside.

2 Place the honey, sugar, and orange flower water in a pan and heat gently until the sugar has dissolved. Bring the mixture to a boil and boil steadily until a temperature of 241°F/116°C has been reached on a sugar thermometer, or a small amount of the mixture forms a soft ball when dropped into cold water.

3 Quickly remove the pan from the heat and stir in the dry ingredients. Mix thoroughly and turn into the prepared pan. Spread evenly and bake in a preheated oven, 325°F/160°C, for 30 minutes. Let cool in the pan. Turn out and carefully peel away the lining paper. Dust confectioners' sugar lightly over the top and cut into wedges to serve.

chocolate tartlets

ingredients

10 oz/275 g ready-made
   sweet pie dough
5^1/$_2$ oz/150 g bittersweet
   chocolate, broken
   into pieces
1^3/$_4$ oz/50 g butter
3^1/$_2$ fl oz/100 ml/scant ^{1}/$_2$ cup
   whipping cream
1 large egg
1 oz/30 g/scant ^{1}/$_8$ cup
   superfine sugar
unsweetened cocoa and
   chocolate curls,
   to decorate
crème fraîche, to serve

method

1 Roll out the pie dough and use to line 4 x 4^1/$_2$-inch/12-cm fluted tart pans with removable bases. Line the pastry shells with waxed paper, then fill with dried beans. Place on a preheated cookie sheet and bake in a preheated oven, 400°F/200°C, for 5 minutes, or until the pastry rims look set. Remove the paper and beans and return the pastry shells to the oven for 5 minutes, or until the bases look dry. Remove from the oven, then let stand on the cookie sheet. Reduce the oven temperature to 350°F/180°C.

2 Meanwhile, place the chocolate in a bowl set over a pan of simmering water so that the bowl does not touch the water. Add the butter and cream and heat until the chocolate and butter melt. Remove from the heat.

3 Beat the egg and sugar together until light and fluffy. Stir the melted chocolate mixture until smooth, then stir it into the egg mixture. Carefully pour the filling into the tart shells, then transfer to the oven and bake for 15 minutes, or until the filling is set and the pastry is golden brown. If the pastry looks as though it is becoming too brown, cover it with foil.

4 Transfer the tartlets to a wire rack to cool completely. Dust with unsweetened cocoa, decorate with chocolate curls, and serve with crème fraîche.

white chocolate tarts

ingredients

MAKES 12

8 oz/225 g/generous 1 cup
   all-purpose flour, plus
   extra for dusting
2 tbsp golden superfine sugar
$5^1/_2$ oz/150 g chilled
   butter, diced
2 egg yolks
2 tbsp cold water
semisweet chocolate curls,
   to decorate (see page 80)
unsweetened cocoa,
   for dusting

filling

1 vanilla bean
14 fl oz/400 ml/$1^3/_4$ cups
   heavy cream
12 oz/350 g white chocolate,
   broken into pieces

method

1 Place the flour and sugar in a bowl. Add the butter and rub it in until the mixture resembles fine bread crumbs. Place the egg yolks and water in a separate bowl and mix together. Stir into the dry ingredients and mix to form a dough. Knead for 1 minute, or until smooth. Wrap in plastic wrap and let chill for 20 minutes.

2 Roll out the dough on a floured counter and use to line 12 tartlet molds. Prick the bases, cover, and let chill for 15 minutes. Line the cases with foil and pie weights and bake in a preheated oven, 400°F/200°C, for 10 minutes. Remove the weights and foil and cook for an additional 5 minutes. Let cool.

3 To make the filling, split the vanilla bean lengthwise and scrape out the black seeds with a knife. Place the seeds in a pan with the cream and heat until almost boiling. Place the chocolate in a heatproof bowl and pour over the hot cream. Keep stirring until smooth. Whisk the mixture with an electric whisk until thickened and the whisk leaves a trail when lifted. Let chill in the refrigerator for 30 minutes, then whisk until soft peaks form. Divide the filling among the pastry shells and let chill for 30 minutes. Decorate with chocolate curls and dust with unsweetened cocoa.

caramel chocolate shortbread

ingredients

MAKES 12

4 oz/115 g butter, plus extra
   for greasing
6 oz/175 g/¾ cup plain flour
2 oz/55 g/⅓ cup golden
   caster sugar

filling and topping

6 oz/175 g butter
4 oz/115 g/⅔ cup golden
   caster sugar
3 tbsp golden syrup
14 oz/400 g canned
   condensed milk
7 oz/200 g plain chocolate,
   broken into pieces

method

1 Grease and line the bottom of a 9-inch/ 23-cm shallow square cake pan. Place the butter, flour, and sugar in a food processor and process until it starts to bind together. Press into the pan and level the top. Bake in a preheated oven, 350°F/180°C, for 20–25 minutes, or until golden.

2 Meanwhile, make the caramel. Place the butter, sugar, syrup, and condensed milk in a heavy-bottom pan. Heat gently until the sugar has melted. Bring to a boil, then reduce the heat and let simmer for 6–8 minutes, stirring, until very thick. Pour over the shortbread and let chill in the refrigerator for 2 hours, or until firm.

3 Melt the chocolate and let cool, then spread over the caramel. Let chill in the refrigerator for 2 hours, or until set. Cut the shortbread into 12 pieces using a sharp knife and serve.

refrigerator cake

ingredients

MAKES 12 PIECES

2 oz/55 g/^{1}/$_3$ cup raisins

2 tbsp brandy

4 oz/115 g semisweet
chocolate, broken
into pieces

4 oz/115 g milk chocolate,
broken into pieces

2 oz/55 g butter, plus extra
for greasing

2 tbsp corn syrup

6 oz/175 g graham crackers,
coarsely broken

2oz/55 g/^{1}/$_2$ cup slivered
almonds, lightly toasted

1 oz/25 g/^{1}/$_8$ cup candied
cherries, chopped

topping

3^1/$_2$ oz/100 g semisweet
chocolate, broken
into pieces

^{3}/$_4$ oz/20 g butter

method

1 Grease and line the bottom of a 7-inch/
18-cm shallow square pan. Place the
raisins and brandy in a bowl and let soak for
30 minutes. Put the chocolate, butter, and
syrup in a pan and heat gently until melted.

2 Stir in the graham crackers, almonds,
cherries, raisins, and brandy. Turn into the
prepared pan and let cool. Cover and let chill
in the refrigerator for 1 hour.

3 To make the topping, place the chocolate
and butter in a small heatproof bowl and melt
over a pan of gently simmering water. Stir and
pour the chocolate mixture over the cookie
base. Let chill in the refrigerator for 8 hours,
or overnight. Cut into bars or squares to serve.

no-bake chocolate squares

ingredients

MAKES 16

9^1/$_2$ oz/275 g semisweet
chocolate

6 oz/175 g butter

4 tbsp golden syrup

2 tbsp dark rum (optional)

6 oz/175 g plain cookies

1 oz/25 g/^{1}/$_3$ cup toasted
rice cereal

1^3/$_4$ oz/50 g/generous ^{1}/$_4$ cup
chopped walnuts
or pecans

3^1/$_2$ oz/100 g/generous
^{1}/$_2$ cup candied cherries,
coarsely chopped

1 oz/25 g white chocolate,
to decorate

method

1 Line a 7-inch/18-cm square cake pan with parchment paper. Place the semisweet chocolate in a large bowl with the butter, syrup, and rum, if using, and set over a pan of gently simmering water until melted, stirring constantly, until blended.

2 Break the cookies into small pieces and stir into the chocolate mixture with the rice cereal, nuts, and cherries.

3 Pour the batter into the pan and level the top, pressing down well with the back of a spoon. Let chill in the refrigerator for 2 hours.

4 To decorate, melt the white chocolate and drizzle it over the top of the cake in a random pattern. Let set. To serve, carefully turn out of the pan and remove the parchment paper. Cut into 16 squares and serve.

chocolate viennese fingers

ingredients

MAKES ABOUT 30

4 oz/115 g butter, softened,
   plus extra for greasing
2 oz/55 g/^{1}/$_2$ cup golden
   confectioners' sugar, sifted
4^1/$_2$ oz/125 g/generous
   ^{3}/$_4$ cup all-purpose flour
1 tbsp unsweetened cocoa
3^1/$_2$ oz/100 g semisweet
   chocolate, melted
   and cooled

method

1 Beat the butter and sugar together until light and fluffy. Sift the flour and unsweetened cocoa into the bowl and work the mixture until it is a smooth, piping consistency.

2 Spoon into a large pastry bag fitted with a 1-inch/2.5-cm fluted tip. Pipe 2^1/$_2$-inch/6-cm lengths of the mixture onto 2 greased baking sheets, allowing room for expansion during cooking. Bake in a preheated oven, 350°F/180°C, for 15 minutes, or until firm.

3 Let cool on the baking sheets for 2 minutes, then transfer to a wire rack to cool completely. Dip the ends of the cookies into the melted chocolate and let set before serving.

double chocolate chip cookies

ingredients

MAKES 12

7 oz/200 g butter, softened, plus extra for greasing

7 oz/200 g/1 cup golden superfine sugar

$^1/_2$ tsp vanilla extract

1 large egg

8 oz/225 g/1$^1/_2$ cups all-purpose flour

pinch of salt

1 tsp baking soda

4 oz/115 g/$^2/_3$ cup white chocolate chips

4 oz/115 g/$^2/_3$ cup semisweet chocolate chips

method

1 Place the butter, sugar, and vanilla extract in a large bowl and beat together. Gradually beat in the egg until the mixture is light and fluffy.

2 Sift the flour, salt, and baking soda over the mixture and fold in. Fold in the chocolate chips. Drop dessertspoonfuls of the mixture onto 3 greased cookie sheets, spaced well apart to allow for spreading during cooking.

3 Bake in a preheated oven, 350°F/180°C, for 10–12 minutes, or until crisp outside but still soft inside. Let cool on the cookie sheets for 2 minutes, then transfer to wire racks to cool completely.

special occasions

This is where you can really give your creative streak a free rein and have endless fun. There are fabulous recipes here to help you celebrate a wedding, a birth, a birthday, an anniversary, or one of the festive occasions in the year.

Children love novelty, so get them involved and make special cupcakes decorated for Easter, Halloween, or Christmas. For their birthday parties, serve Birthday Party Cupcakes, Lemon Butterfly Cakes, Gingerbread People, and Party Cookies decorated with colorful sugar-coated chocolate beans—these will render the party guests speechless just long enough for you to catch your breath!

When romance is in the air, make Valentine Heart Cupcakes for your loved one, or use a cookie cutter to shape Vanilla Hearts. A cupcake-cake is perfect for an informal wedding, and to celebrate both weddings and the subsequent anniversaries, choose Rose Petal Muffins and Cupcakes and Strawberry Rose Meringues—they look, and taste, absolutely stunning. And for a baby shower—cakes with pale pink and pale blue frosting, of course!

For an adult birthday party or just a get-together, be a little different and serve muffins laced with your favorite liqueur—brandy, Amaretto, Cointreau, the choice is yours.

rose petal muffins

ingredients

MAKES 12

1 tbsp sunflower or peanut
   oil, for oiling (if using)
8 oz/225 g/1^1/$_2$ cups
   all-purpose flour
2 tsp baking powder
pinch of salt
4 tbsp butter
6 tbsp superfine sugar
1 large egg, beaten
4 fl oz/110 ml/^{1}/$_2$ cup milk
1 tsp rose water
1^3/$_4$ oz/50 g edible rose
   petals, rinsed, patted dry,
   and lightly snipped

rose petal frosting

3^1/$_2$ oz/100 g/ scant 1 cup
   confectioners' sugar
1 tbsp liquid glucose
1 tbsp rose water
1^3/$_4$ oz/50 g edible
   rose petals, rinsed
   and patted dry

method

1 Oil a 12-cup muffin pan with sunflower oil, or line it with 12 muffin paper liners. Sift the flour, baking powder, and salt into a large mixing bowl.

2 In a separate large bowl, cream together the butter and superfine sugar, then stir in the beaten egg, milk, rose water, and snipped rose petals. Add the butter mixture to the flour mixture and then gently stir together until just combined. Do not overstir the batter—it is fine for it to be a little lumpy.

3 Divide the muffin batter evenly among the 12 cups in the muffin pan or the paper liners (they should be about two-thirds full). Transfer to a preheated oven, 400°F/200°C, and bake for 20 minutes, or until risen and golden.

4 While the muffins are cooking, make the frosting. Place the confectioners' sugar in a bowl, then stir in the liquid glucose and rose water. Cover with plastic wrap until ready to use.

5 When the muffins are cooked, remove them from the oven, place on a cooling rack, and let cool. When they have cooled, spread each muffin with some of the frosting, strew over and/or around with the rose petals, and serve.

frosted lavender muffins

ingredients

MAKES 12

1 large baking apple, peeled, cored, and thinly sliced

3 tbsp water

5 oz/150 g/1 cup all-purpose flour

1 tsp baking powder

1 tsp baking soda

pinch of salt

4 tbsp butter

4 tbsp superfine sugar

1 large egg, beaten

$1/2$ tsp vanilla extract

1 tbsp dried lavender flowers, stripped from their stalks

lavender frosting

$3^1/2$ oz/100 g/scant 1 cup confectioners' sugar

1 tbsp dried lavender flowers

1 tbsp liquid glucose

1–2 tbsp milk

method

1 The day before you make the muffins, place the confectioners' sugar in a bowl, then add the dried lavender flowers. Cover with plastic wrap and leave overnight until ready for use.

2 To make the muffins, place the sliced apple and water in a pan and bring to a boil, then cover and let simmer for 15–20 minutes, stirring occasionally, until the water has been absorbed. Remove from the heat and let cool. Process in a food processor until smooth.

3 Line a 12-cup muffin pan with muffin paper liners. Sift the flour, baking powder, baking soda, and salt into a mixing bowl. In a separate bowl, cream together the butter and superfine sugar, then stir in the beaten egg, vanilla extract, apple purée, and dried lavender flowers. Gently stir the egg mixture into the flour mixture until just combined. Do not overstir the batter—it is fine for it to be a little lumpy.

4 Divide the muffin batter among the paper liners (they should be about two-thirds full). Transfer to a preheated oven, 400°F/ 200°C, and bake for 20 minutes, or until risen and golden. Let cool completely on a wire rack.

5 To finish making the frosting, sift the sugar/ lavender mixture into a bowl and discard the flowers. Stir in the liquid glucose and enough milk to make the frosting easy to spread. Spread each muffin with frosting and serve.

irish coffee muffins

ingredients

MAKES 12

1 tbsp sunflower or peanut
   oil, for oiling (if using)
10 oz/275 g/2 cups
   all-purpose flour
1 tbsp baking powder
pinch of salt
3 oz/85 g butter
2 oz/55 g/scant $^1/_2$ cup
   raw sugar
1 large egg, beaten
4 fl oz/125 ml/$^1/_2$ cup
   heavy cream
1 tsp almond extract
2 tbsp strong coffee
2 tbsp coffee-flavored liqueur
4 tbsp Irish whiskey or
   similar whiskey
whipped heavy cream,
   to serve (optional)

method

1 Oil a 12-cup muffin pan with sunflower oil, or line it with 12 muffin paper liners. Sift the flour, baking powder, and salt into a large mixing bowl.

2 In a separate large bowl, cream the butter and raw sugar together, then stir in the beaten egg. Pour in the heavy cream, almond extract, coffee, liqueur, and whiskey and stir together. Add the whiskey mixture to the flour mixture and then gently stir together until just combined. Do not overstir the batter—it is fine for it to be a little lumpy.

3 Divide the muffin batter evenly among the 12 cups in the muffin pan or the paper liners (they should be about two-thirds full). Transfer to a preheated oven, 400°F/200°C, and bake for 20 minutes, or until risen and golden. Remove the muffins from the oven and serve warm, or place them on a cooling rack and let cool. If liked, fill the muffins with whipped heavy cream, to serve.

mocha muffins

ingredients

MAKES 12

1 tbsp sunflower or peanut
oil, for oiling (if using)

9 oz/250 g/generous
1³/₄ cups all-purpose flour

1 tbsp baking powder

2 tbsp unsweetened cocoa

pinch of salt

4 oz/115 g butter, melted

5¹/₂ oz/150 g/scant
³/₄ cup raw sugar

1 large egg, beaten

4 fl oz/110 ml/1 cup milk

1 tsp almond extract

2 tbsp strong coffee

1 tbsp instant coffee powder

2 oz/115 g/generous ¹/₄ cup
semisweet chocolate chips

1 oz/25 g/scant ¹/₃ cup raisins

cocoa topping

3 tbsp raw sugar

1 tbsp unsweetened cocoa

1 tsp allspice

method

1 Oil a 12-cup muffin pan with sunflower oil, or line it with 12 muffin paper liners. Sift the flour, baking powder, cocoa, and salt into a large mixing bowl.

2 In a separate large bowl, cream the butter and raw sugar together, then stir in the beaten egg. Pour in the milk, almond extract, and coffee, then add the coffee powder, chocolate chips, and raisins and gently mix together. Add the raisin mixture to the flour mixture and gently stir together until just combined. Do not overstir the batter—it is fine for it to be a little lumpy.

3 Divide the muffin batter evenly among the 12 cups in the muffin pan or the paper liners (they should be about two-thirds full). To make the topping, place the raw sugar in a bowl, add the cocoa and allspice, and mix together well. Sprinkle the topping over the muffins, then transfer to a preheated oven, 375°F/190°C, and bake for 20 minutes, or until risen and golden. Remove the muffins from the oven and serve warm, or place them on a cooling rack and let cool.

triple chocolate muffins

ingredients

MAKES 12

9 oz/250 g/generous 1³/₄ cups all-purpose flour

1 oz/25 g/¹/₃ cup unsweetened cocoa

2 tsp baking powder

¹/₂ tsp baking soda

3¹/₂ oz/100 g/generous ¹/₂ cup semisweet chocolate chips

3¹/₂ oz/100 g/generous ¹/₂ cup white chocolate chips

2 large eggs, beaten

10 fl oz/300 ml/1¹/₄ cups sour cream

3 oz/85 g/scant ¹/₂ cup packed brown sugar

3 oz/85 g butter, melted

method

1 Line a 12-cup muffin pan with muffin paper liners. Sift the flour, cocoa, baking powder, and baking soda into a large bowl, add the semisweet and white chocolate chips, and stir.

2 Place the eggs, sour cream, sugar, and melted butter in a separate mixing bowl and mix well. Add the wet ingredients to the dry ingredients and stir gently until just combined.

3 Divide the batter among the paper liners and bake in a preheated oven, 400°F/ 200°C, for 20 minutes, or until well risen and firm to the touch. Remove from the oven and serve warm, or place on a cooling rack and let cool.

rice muffins with amaretto

ingredients

MAKES 9

butter, for greasing

5 oz/150 g/1 cup
   all-purpose flour

1 tbsp baking powder

$1/2$ tsp baking soda

$1/2$ tsp salt

1 large egg

4 tbsp honey

4 fl oz/110 ml/$1/2$ cup milk

2 tbsp sunflower
   or peanut oil

$1/2$ tsp almond extract

2 oz/55 g/$3/4$ cup
   cooked risotto rice

2–3 amaretti cookies,
   coarsely crushed

Amaretto butter

1 tbsp honey

1–2 tbsp Amaretto

$3^1/2$ oz/100 g/$1/2$ cup
   mascarpone cheese

method

1 Grease 9 cups of a 12-cup muffin pan with butter. Sift the flour, baking powder, baking soda, and salt into a large bowl and stir. Make a well in the center.

2 In a separate bowl, beat the egg, honey, milk, oil, and almond extract with an electric whisk for about 2 minutes, or until light and foamy. Gradually beat in the rice. Pour into the well in the dry ingredients and, using a fork, stir lightly until just combined.

3 Divide the batter evenly among the 9 cups in the muffin pan. Sprinkle each muffin with amaretti crumbs and bake in a preheated oven, 400°F/200°C, for 15 minutes until risen and golden. The tops should spring back when pressed. Remove from the oven and cool in the pan for about 1 minute. Carefully remove the muffins and let cool slightly.

4 To make the Amaretto butter, place the honey, Amaretto, and mascarpone in a small bowl and beat together. Spoon into a small serving bowl and serve with the warm muffins.

brandied cherry muffins

ingredients

MAKES 12

1 tbsp sunflower or peanut
   oil, for oiling (if using)
8 oz/225 g/generous
   1 1/2 cups all-purpose flour
1 tbsp baking powder
pinch of salt
3 tbsp butter
2 tbsp superfine sugar
1 large egg, beaten
7 fl oz/200 ml/scant
   1 cup milk
2 tsp cherry brandy
10 1/2 oz/300 g drained
   canned cherries, chopped

method

1 Oil a 12-cup muffin pan with sunflower oil, or line it with 12 muffin paper liners. Sift the flour, baking powder, and salt into a large mixing bowl.

2 In a separate large bowl, cream the butter and superfine sugar together, then stir in the beaten egg. Pour in the milk and cherry brandy, then add the chopped cherries and gently stir together. Add the cherry mixture to the flour mixture and then gently stir together until just combined. Do not overstir the batter—it is fine for it to be a little lumpy.

3 Divide the muffin batter among the 12 cups in the muffin pan or the paper liners (they should be about two-thirds full). Transfer to a preheated oven, 400°F/200°C, and bake for 20–25 minutes until risen and golden. Remove from the oven and serve warm, or place them on a cooling rack and let cool.

apricot muffins with cointreau

ingredients

MAKES 12

1 tbsp sunflower or peanut
    oil, for oiling (if using)

$4^1/_2$ oz/125 g/scant 1 cup
    self-rising flour

2 tsp baking powder

6 oz/175 g butter

$4^1/_2$ oz/125 g/scant $^2/_3$ cup
    superfine sugar

2 large eggs, beaten

4 fl oz/110 ml/$^1/_2$ cup milk

4 tbsp light cream

1 tbsp orange-flavored
    liqueur, such as Cointreau

3 oz/85 g/generous $^1/_2$ cup
    no-soak dried
    apricots, chopped

3 oz/85 g/generous $^1/_2$ cup
    no-soak dried dates,
    pitted and chopped

cinnamon topping

3 tbsp raw sugar

1 tsp ground cinnamon

1 tbsp freshly grated
    orange rind

method

1 Oil a 12-cup muffin pan with sunflower oil, or line it with 12 muffin paper liners.

2 Sift the flour and baking powder into a large mixing bowl.

3 In a separate large bowl, cream together the butter and superfine sugar, then stir in the beaten eggs. Pour in the milk, cream, and orange-flavored liqueur, then add the chopped apricots and dates and gently mix together. Add the fruit mixture to the flour mixture and then gently stir together until just combined. Do not overstir the batter—it is fine for it to be a little lumpy.

4 Divide the muffin batter evenly among the 12 cups in the muffin pan or the paper liners (they should be about two-thirds full). To make the topping, place the raw sugar in a small bowl, then mix in the cinnamon and orange rind. Sprinkle the topping over the muffins, then transfer to the oven and bake in a preheated oven, 375°F/190°C, for 20 minutes, or until risen and golden. Remove the muffins from the oven and serve warm, or place them on a cooling rack and let cool.

marshmallow muffins

ingredients

MAKES 12

$2^1/_2$ oz/70 g butter

10 oz/275 g/2 cups
  all-purpose flour

6 tbsp unsweetened cocoa

3 tsp baking powder

3 oz/85 g/scant $^1/_2$ cup
  superfine sugar

$3^1/_2$ oz/100 g/generous $^1/_2$
  cup milk chocolate chips

2 oz/55 g/$^1/_4$ cup multicolored
  mini marshmallows

1 large egg, beaten

10 fl oz/300 ml/$1^1/_4$ cups milk

method

1 Line a 12-cup muffin pan with muffin paper liners. Melt the butter in a pan.

2 Sift the flour, cocoa, and baking powder together into a large bowl. Stir in the sugar, chocolate chips, and marshmallows until thoroughly mixed.

3 Whisk the egg, milk, and melted butter together in a separate bowl, then gently stir into the flour to form a stiff batter. Divide the batter evenly among the muffin liners.

4 Bake in a preheated oven, 375°F/190°C, for 20–25 minutes until well risen and golden brown. Remove from the oven and let cool in the pan for 5 minutes, then place on a cooling rack and let cool completely.

easter cupcakes

ingredients

MAKES 12

8 tbsp butter, softened,
   or soft margarine
4 oz/115 g/generous $^1/_2$ cup
   superfine sugar
2 eggs, lightly beaten
3 oz/85 g/generous $^1/_2$ cup
   self-rising white flour
1 oz/25 g/generous $^1/_4$ cup
   unsweetened cocoa

topping

6 tbsp butter, softened
6 oz/175 g/1$^1/_2$ cups
   confectioners' sugar
1 tbsp milk
2–3 drops of vanilla extract
36 mini chocolate candy
   shell eggs

method

1 Put 12 paper baking cases in a muffin pan, or place 12 double-layer paper cases on a cookie sheet.

2 Put the butter and sugar in a bowl and beat together until light and fluffy. Gradually add the eggs, beating well after each addition. Sift in the flour and cocoa and, using a large metal spoon, fold into the mixture. Spoon the batter into the paper cases.

3 Bake the cupcakes in a preheated oven, 350°F/180°C, for 15–20 minutes, or until well risen and firm to the touch. Transfer to a wire rack and let cool.

4 To make the buttercream topping, put the butter in a bowl and beat until fluffy. Sift in the confectioners' sugar and beat together until well mixed, adding the milk and vanilla extract.

5 When the cupcakes are cold, put the frosting in a pastry bag, fitted with a large star tip, and pipe a circle around the edge of each cupcake to form a nest. Place 3 chocolate eggs in the center of each nest, to decorate.

halloween cupcakes

ingredients

MAKES 12

8 tbsp soft margarine

4 oz/115 g/generous $^1/_2$ cup
  superfine sugar

2 eggs

4 oz/115 g/generous $^3/_4$ cup
  self-rising white flour

topping

7 oz/200 g orange
  ready-to-roll colored
  fondant frosting

confectioners' sugar,
  for dusting

2 oz/55 g black ready-to-roll
  colored fondant frosting

black cake writing frosting

white cake writing frosting

method

1 Put 12 paper baking cases in a muffin pan, or place 12 double-layer paper cases on a cookie sheet.

2 Put the margarine, sugar, eggs, and flour in a bowl and, using an electric hand whisk, beat together until smooth. Spoon the batter into the cases.

3 Bake the cupcakes in a preheated oven, 350°F/180°C, for 15–20 minutes, or until well risen, golden brown, and firm to the touch. Transfer to a wire rack and let cool.

4 Knead the orange frosting until pliable, then roll out on a counter dusted with confectioners' sugar. Using the palm of your hand, lightly rub confectioners' sugar into the frosting to prevent it from spotting. Using a 2$^1/_4$-inch/5.5-cm plain round cutter, cut out 12 circles, re-rolling the frosting as necessary. Place a circle on top of each cupcake.

5 Roll out the black frosting on a counter lightly dusted with confectioners' sugar. Using the palm of your hand, lightly rub confectioners' sugar into the frosting to prevent it from spotting. Using a 1$^1/_4$-inch/3-cm plain round cutter, cut out 12 circles and place them on the center of the cupcakes. Using black writing frosting, pipe 8 legs on to each spider and using white writing frosting, draw 2 eyes and a mouth.

christmas cupcakes

ingredients

MAKES 16

9 tbsp butter, softened

7 oz/200 g/1 cup
   superfine sugar

4–6 drops almond extract

4 eggs, lightly beaten

5^1/2 oz/150 g/generous 1 cup
   self-rising white flour

6 oz/175 g/1^3/4 cups
   ground almonds

topping

1 lb/450 g white ready-to-roll
   fondant frosting

2 oz/55 g green ready-to-roll
   colored fondant frosting

1 oz/25 g red ready-to-roll
   colored fondant frosting

confectioners' sugar,
   for dusting

method

1 Put 16 paper muffin cases in a muffin pan.

2 Put the butter, sugar, and almond extract in a bowl and beat together until light and fluffy. Gradually add the eggs, beating well after each addition. Add the flour and, using a large metal spoon, fold it into the mixture, then fold in the ground almonds. Spoon the batter into the paper cases to half-fill them.

3 Bake the cakes in a preheated oven, 350°F/180°C, for 20 minutes, or until well risen, golden brown, and firm to the touch. Transfer to a wire rack and let cool.

4 When the cakes are cold, knead the white frosting until pliable, then roll out on a counter lightly dusted with confectioners' sugar. Using a 2^3/4-inch/7-cm plain round cutter, cut out 16 circles, re-rolling the frosting as necessary. Place a circle on top of each cupcake.

5 Roll out the green frosting on a counter lightly dusted with confectioners' sugar. Using the palm of your hand, rub confectioners' sugar into the frosting to prevent it from spotting. Using a holly leaf-shaped cutter, cut out 32 leaves, rerolling the frosting as necessary. Brush each leaf with a little cooled boiled water and place 2 leaves on top of each cake. Roll the red frosting between the palms of your hands to form 48 berries and place in the center of the leaves.

valentine heart cupcakes

ingredients

MAKES 6

6 tbsp butter, softened, or soft
    margarine
3 oz/85 g/scant $1/2$ cup
    superfine sugar
$1/2$ tsp vanilla extract
2 eggs, lightly beaten
$2^{1}/2$ oz/70 g/$1/2$ cup
    all-purpose flour
1 tbsp unsweetened cocoa
1 tsp baking powder

marzipan hearts

$1^{1}/4$ oz/35 g marzipan
red food coloring (liquid
    or paste)
confectioners' sugar,
    for dusting

topping

4 tbsp butter, softened
4 oz/115 g/1 cup
    confectioners' sugar
1 oz/25 g semisweet
    chocolate, melted
6 chocolate flower
    decorations

method

1 To make the hearts, knead the marzipan until pliable, then add a few drops of red coloring and knead until evenly colored red. Roll out the marzipan to a thickness of $1/4$ inch/5 mm on a counter dusted with confectioners' sugar. Using a small heart-shaped cutter, cut out 6 hearts. Place on a tray lined with waxed paper and dusted with confectioners' sugar. Let dry for 3–4 hours.

2 Put 6 paper muffin cases in a muffin pan.

3 Put the butter, sugar, and vanilla extract in a bowl and beat together until light and fluffy. Gradually add the eggs, beating well after each addition. Sift in the flour, cocoa, and baking powder and, using a large metal spoon, fold into the mixture. Spoon the batter into the paper cases.

4 Bake the cupcakes in a preheated oven, 350°F/180°C, for 20–25 minutes, or until well risen and firm to the touch. Transfer to a wire rack and let cool.

5 To make the topping, put the butter in a large bowl and beat until fluffy. Sift in the confectioners' sugar and beat together until smooth. Add the melted chocolate and beat together until well mixed. When the cakes are cold, spread the frosting on top of each cake and decorate with a chocolate flower.

cupcake wedding cake

ingredients

MAKES 48

1 lb/450 g butter, softened

1 lb/450 g/2 cups
    superfine sugar

2 tsp vanilla extract

8 large eggs, lightly beaten

1 lb/450 g/4 cups self-rising
    white flour

5 fl oz/150 ml/²/₃ cup milk

topping

1 lb 4 oz/550 g/5 cups
    confectioners' sugar

48 ready-made sugar roses,
    or 48 small fresh rosebuds
    gently rinsed and left to
    dry on paper towels

to assemble the cake

one 20-inch/50-cm, one
    16-inch/40-cm, one
    12-inch/30-cm, and one
    8-inch/20-cm sandblasted
    glass disk with polished
    edges, or 4 silver
    cake boards

13 white or Perspex cake pillars

1 small bouquet of fresh
    flowers in a small vase

method

1 Put 48 paper baking cases in a muffin pan, or place 48 double-layer paper cases on a cookie sheet.

2 Put the butter, sugar, and vanilla extract in a bowl and beat together until light and fluffy. Gradually add the eggs, beating well after each addition. Add the flour and, using a large metal spoon, fold into the mixture with the milk. Spoon the batter into the paper cases.

3 Bake the cupcakes in a preheated oven, 350°F/180°C, for 15–20 minutes, or until well risen and firm to the touch. Transfer to a wire rack and let cool.

4 To make the topping, sift the confectioners' sugar into a large bowl. Add 3–4 tablespoons hot water and stir until the mixture is smooth and thick enough to coat the back of a wooden spoon. Spoon on top of each cupcake. Store in an airtight container for up to one day.

5 On the day of serving, carefully place a sugar rose or rosebud on top of each cupcake. To arrange the cupcakes, place the largest disk or board on a table where the finished display is to be. Stand 5 pillars on the disk and arrange some of the cupcakes on the base. Continue with the remaining bases, pillars (using only 4 pillars to support each remaining tier), and cupcakes to make 4 tiers, standing the bouquet of flowers in the center of the top tier.

rose petal cupcakes

ingredients

MAKES 12

8 tbsp butter, softened

4 oz/115 g/generous $^1/_2$ cup
superfine sugar

2 eggs, lightly beaten

1 tbsp milk

few drops of extract of rose oil

$^1/_4$ tsp vanilla extract

6 oz/175 g/scant $1^1/_4$ cups
self-rising white flour

frosting

6 tbsp butter, softened

6 oz/175 g/$1^1/_2$ cups
confectioners' sugar

pink or purple food coloring
(optional)

silver dragées (cake decoration
balls), to decorate

candied rose petals

12–24 rose petals

lightly beaten egg white,
for brushing

superfine sugar, for sprinkling

method

1 To make the candied rose petals, gently rinse the petals and dry well with paper towels. Using a pastry brush, paint both sides of a rose petal with egg white, then coat well with superfine sugar. Place on a tray and repeat with the remaining petals. Cover the tray with foil and let dry overnight.

2 Put 12 paper baking cases in a muffin pan, or place 12 double-layer paper cases on a cookie sheet.

3 Put the butter and sugar in a bowl and beat together until light and fluffy. Gradually add the eggs, beating well after each addition. Stir in the milk, rose oil extract, and vanilla extract then, using a metal spoon, fold in the flour. Spoon the batter into the paper cases.

4 Bake the cupcakes in a preheated oven, 400°F/200°C, for 12–15 minutes until well risen and golden brown. Transfer to a wire rack and let cool.

5 To make the frosting, put the butter in a large bowl and beat until fluffy. Sift in the confectioners' sugar and mix well together. If wished, add a few drops of pink or purple food coloring to complement the rose petals.

6 When the cupcakes are cold, spread the frosting on top of each cake. Top with 1–2 candied rose petals and sprinkle with silver dragées to decorate.

baby shower cupcakes

ingredients

MAKES 24

14 oz/400 g/1³/₄ cups
   butter, softened
14 oz/400 g/2 cups
   superfine sugar
finely grated rind of 2 lemons
8 eggs, lightly beaten
14 oz/400 g/generous
   2³/₄ cups self-rising
   white flour

topping

12 oz/350 g/3 cups
   confectioners' sugar
red or blue food coloring
   (liquid or paste)
24 sugared almonds

method

1 Put 24 paper muffin cases in a muffin pan.

2 Put the butter, sugar, and lemon rind in a bowl and beat together until light and fluffy. Gradually add the eggs, beating well after each addition. Add the flour and, using a large metal spoon, fold into the mixture. Spoon the batter into the paper cases to half-fill them.

3 Bake the cupcakes in a preheated oven, 350°F/180°C, for 20–25 minutes, or until well risen, golden brown, and firm to the touch. Transfer to a wire rack and let cool.

4 When the cakes are cold, make the topping. Sift the confectioners' sugar into a bowl. Add 6–8 teaspoons of hot water and stir until the mixture is smooth and thick enough to coat the back of a wooden spoon. Dip a skewer into the red or blue food coloring, then stir it into the frosting until it is evenly colored pink or pale blue.

5 Spoon the frosting on top of each cupcake. Top each with a sugared almond and let set for about 30 minutes before serving.

birthday party cupcakes

ingredients

MAKES 24

8 oz/225 g/1 cup
   soft margarine
8 oz/225 g/scant 1¼ cups
   superfine sugar
4 eggs
8 oz/225 g/generous
   1½ cups self-rising
   white flour

topping

6 oz/175 g/¾ cup
   butter, softened
12 oz/350 g/3 cups
   confectioners' sugar
a variety of edible sugar
   flower shapes, cake
   decorating sprinkles, silver
   dragées (cake decoration
   balls), and sugar strands
various colored tubes of
   writing frosting
24 birthday cake candles
   (optional)
silver dragées (cake
   decoration balls)

method

1 Put 24 paper baking cases in a muffin pan, or place 24 double-layer paper cases on a cookie sheet.

2 Put the margarine, sugar, eggs, and flour in a large bowl and, using an electric hand whisk, beat together until just smooth. Spoon the batter into the paper cases.

3 Bake the cupcakes in a preheated oven, 350°F/180°C, for 15–20 minutes, or until well risen, golden brown, and firm to the touch. Transfer to a wire rack and let cool.

4 To make the frosting, put the butter in a bowl and beat until fluffy. Sift in the confectioners' sugar and beat together until smooth and creamy. When the cupcakes are cold, spread the frosting on top of each cupcake, then decorate to your choice and, if desired, place a candle in the top of each.

gold & silver anniversary cupcakes

ingredients

MAKES 24

8 oz/225 g/1 cup
    butter, softened
8 oz/225 g/generous 1 cup
    superfine sugar
1 tsp vanilla extract
4 large eggs, lightly beaten
8 oz/225 g/generous
    1½ cups self-rising
    white flour
5 tbsp milk

topping

6 oz/175 g/¾ cup
    unsalted butter
12 oz/350 g/3 cups
    confectioners' sugar
silver or gold dragées (cake
    decoration balls)

method

1 Put 24 silver or gold foil cake cases in muffin pans, or arrange them on baking sheets.

2 Put the butter, sugar, and vanilla extract in a bowl and beat together until light and fluffy. Gradually add the eggs, beating well after each addition. Add the flour and, using a large metal spoon, fold into the mixture with the milk. Spoon the batter into the paper cases.

3 Bake the cupcakes in a preheated oven, 350°F/180°C, for 15–20 minutes, or until well risen and firm to the touch. Transfer to a wire rack and let cool.

4 To make the topping, put the butter in a large bowl and beat until fluffy. Sift in the confectioners' sugar and beat together until well mixed. Put the topping in a pastry bag, fitted with a medium star-shaped tip.

5 When the cupcakes are cold, pipe icing on top of each. Sprinkle over the silver or gold dragées before serving.

feather-frosted coffee cupcakes

ingredients

MAKES 16

1 tbsp instant coffee granules

1 tbsp boiling water

8 tbsp butter, softened,
   or soft margarine

4 oz/115 g/generous $^1/_2$ cup
   firmly packed brown sugar

2 eggs

4 oz/115 g/generous $^3/_4$ cup
   self-rising white flour

$^1/_2$ tsp baking powder

2 tbsp sour cream

frosting

8 oz/225 g/2 cups
   confectioners' sugar

4 tsp warm water

1 tsp instant coffee granules

2 tsp boiling water

method

1 Put 16 paper baking cases in a muffin pan, or place 16 double-layer paper cases on a cookie sheet.

2 Put the coffee granules in a cup or small bowl, add the boiling water, and stir until dissolved. Let cool slightly.

3 Put the butter, sugar, and eggs in a bowl. Sift in the flour and baking powder, then beat the ingredients together until smooth. Add the dissolved coffee and the sour cream and beat together until well mixed. Spoon the batter into the paper cases. Bake in a preheated oven, 375°F/190°C, for 20 minutes, or until well risen and golden brown. Transfer to a wire rack and let cool.

4 To make the frosting, sift $^3/_4$ cup of the confectioners' sugar into a bowl, then gradually mix in the warm water to make a coating consistency that will cover the back of a wooden spoon. Dissolve the coffee granules in the boiling water. Sift the remaining confectioners' sugar into a bowl, then stir in the dissolved coffee granules. Spoon the frosting into a pastry bag fitted with a piping tip. When the cupcakes are cold, coat the tops with the white frosting, then quickly pipe the coffee frosting in parallel lines on top. Using a skewer, draw it across the piped lines in both directions. Let set before serving.

lavender fairy cakes

ingredients

MAKES 12

4 oz/115 g/generous $^1\!/_2$ cup
   golden superfine sugar
4 oz/115 g butter, softened
2 eggs, beaten
1 tbsp milk
1 tsp finely chopped lavender
   flowers
$^1\!/_2$ tsp vanilla extract
6 oz/175 g/1$^1\!/_4$ cups self-rising
   flour, sifted
5 oz/150 g/scant 1$^1\!/_2$ cups
   confectioners' sugar

to decorate

lavender flowers
silver dragées

method

1 Place 12 paper cake cases in a muffin pan. Place the superfine sugar and butter in a bowl and cream together until pale and fluffy. Gradually beat in the eggs. Stir in the milk, lavender, and vanilla extract, then carefully fold in the flour.

2 Divide the mixture among the paper cases and bake in a preheated oven, 400°F/200°C, for 12–15 minutes, or until well risen and golden. The sponge should bounce back when pressed.

3 A few minutes before the cakes are ready, sift the confectioners' sugar into a bowl and stir in enough water to make a thick frosting.

4 When the fairy cakes are baked, transfer to a wire rack and place a blob of frosting in the center of each one, allowing it to run across the cake. Decorate with lavender flowers and silver dragées and serve as soon as the cakes are cool.

lemon butterfly cakes

ingredients

MAKES 12

4 oz/115 g/generous ³/₄ cup
    self-rising white flour
¹/₂ tsp baking powder
8 tbsp soft margarine
4 oz/115 g/generous ¹/₂ cup
    superfine sugar
2 eggs, lightly beaten
finely grated rind of ¹/₂ lemon
2 tbsp milk
confectioners' sugar,
    for dusting

lemon filling

6 tbsp butter, softened
6 oz/175 g/1¹/₂ cups
    confectioners' sugar
1 tbsp lemon juice

method

1 Put 12 paper baking cases in a muffin pan, or place 12 double-layer paper cases on a cookie sheet.

2 Sift the flour and baking powder into a large bowl. Add the margarine, sugar, eggs, lemon rind, and milk and, using an electric hand whisk, beat together until smooth. Spoon the batter into the paper cases.

3 Bake the cupcakes in a preheated oven, 375°F/190°C, for 15–20 minutes, or until well risen and golden brown. Transfer to a wire rack and let cool.

4 To make the filling, put the butter in a bowl and beat until fluffy. Sift in the confectioners' sugar, add the lemon juice, and beat together until smooth and creamy.

5 When the cupcakes are cold, use a serrated knife to cut a circle from the top of each cupcake and then cut each circle in half. Spread or pipe a little of the buttercream filling into the center of each cupcake, then press the 2 semicircular halves into it at an angle to resemble butterfly wings. Dust with sifted confectioners' sugar before serving.

strawberry rose meringues

ingredients

MAKES 12

2 egg whites

4 oz/115 g/generous $^1/_2$ cup
superfine sugar

filling

2 oz/55 g/$^1/_3$ cup strawberries

2 tsp confectioners' sugar

3 tbsp rose water

5 fl oz/150 ml/$^2/_3$ cup
heavy cream

to decorate

12 fresh strawberries

rose petals

method

1 Line 2 large cookie sheets with nonstick parchment paper. Place the egg whites in a large, spotlessly clean, greasefree bowl and whisk until stiff peaks form. Whisk in half the sugar, then carefully fold in the remainder.

2 Spoon the meringue into a pastry bag fitted with a large star nozzle. Make 24 x 3-inch/ 7.5-cm lengths onto the cookie sheets. Bake in a preheated oven, 225°F/110°C, for 1 hour, or until the meringues are dry and crisp. Cool on wire racks.

3 To make the filling, place the strawberries in a blender or food processor and process to a purée. Strain the purée into a bowl and stir in the confectioners' sugar and rose water. Place the cream in a separate bowl and whip until thick. Stir into the strawberry mixture and mix well together.

4 Fill the meringues with the strawberry cream. Cut 6 of the strawberries for the decoration in half and use to decorate the meringues. Scatter rose petals over the top and serve at once with the remaining whole strawberries.

zuccherini

ingredients

MAKES 12

6 oz/175 g semisweet
  chocolate, broken
  into pieces
10 amaretti cookies, crushed

mousse

2 oz/55 g semisweet chocolate,
  broken into pieces
1 tbsp cold, strong black coffee
2 eggs, separated
2 tsp orange-flavored liqueur

to decorate

5 fl oz/150 ml/^{2}/$_3$ cup
  heavy cream
2 tbsp unsweetened cocoa
6 chocolate-coated
  coffee beans

method

1 To make the chocolate cups to hold the filling, put the 6-oz/175-g semisweet chocolate into a heatproof bowl set over a pan of barely simmering water. Stir until melted and smooth, but not too runny, then remove the chocolate from the heat. Carefully coat the inside of 12 double paper cake cases with melted chocolate, using a small brush. Stand the chocolate cups on a plate and let chill for at least 8 hours or overnight in the refrigerator.

2 To make the mousse, put the chocolate and coffee into a heatproof bowl set over a pan of barely simmering water. Stir over low heat until the chocolate has melted and the mixture is smooth, then remove from the heat. Let cool slightly, then stir in the egg yolks and liqueur.

3 Whisk the egg whites in a separate bowl until stiff peaks form. Fold into the chocolate mixture with a metal spoon, then let cool.

4 Remove the chocolate cups from the refrigerator and carefully peel off the paper cases. Divide the crushed amaretti cookies equally among the chocolate cups and top with the chocolate mousse. Return to the refrigerator for at least 30 minutes. Just before serving, whip the cream and pipe a star on the top of each chocolate cup. Dust half of the zuccherini with unsweetened cocoa and decorate the other half with chocolate-coated coffee beans.

vanilla hearts

ingredients

MAKES 12

8 oz/225 g/1¹/₂ cups
  all-purpose flour, plus
  extra for dusting
5¹/₂ oz/150 g butter, cut into
  small pieces, plus extra
  for greasing
4¹/₂ oz/125 g/³/₄ cups
  superfine sugar, plus
  extra for dusting
1 tsp vanilla extract

method

1 Sift the flour into a large bowl. Add the butter and rub it in with your fingertips until the mixture resembles fine bread crumbs. Stir in the superfine sugar and vanilla extract and mix together to form a firm dough.

2 Roll out the dough on a lightly floured counter to a thickness of 1 inch/2.5 cm. Stamp out 12 hearts with a heart-shaped cookie cutter measuring 2 inches/5 cm across and 1 inch/2.5 cm deep. Arrange the hearts on a lightly greased cookie sheet.

3 Bake in a preheated oven, 350°F/180°C, for 15–20 minutes, or until the hearts are a light golden color. Transfer the vanilla hearts to a wire rack and let cool completely. Dust them with a little superfine sugar just before serving.

gingerbread people

ingredients

MAKES 20,
USING LARGE CUTTERS

1 lb/450 g/3^1/2 cups all-
purpose flour, plus extra
for dusting

2 tsp ground ginger

1 tsp allspice

2 tsp baking soda

4 oz/115 g/^{1}/2 cup butter,
plus extra for greasing

3^1/2 oz/100 g/generous
^{1}/3 cup corn syrup

4 oz/115 g/generous ^{1}/2 cup
brown sugar

1 egg, beaten

to decorate

currants

candied cherries

3 oz/85 g/generous ^{3}/4 cup
confectioners' sugar

3–4 tsp water

method

1 Sift the flour, ginger, allspice, and baking soda into a large bowl. Place the butter, syrup, and sugar in a pan over low heat and stir until melted. Pour onto the dry ingredients and add the egg. Mix together to form a dough. The dough will be sticky to start with, but will become firmer as it cools.

2 On a lightly floured counter, roll out the dough to about ^{1}/8-inch/3-mm thick and stamp out gingerbread people shapes. Place on 3 large, greased cookie sheets. Re-knead and re-roll the trimmings and cut out more shapes until the dough is used up. Decorate with currants for eyes and pieces of cherry for mouths. Bake in a preheated oven, 325°F/160°C, for 15–20 minutes, or until firm and lightly browned.

3 Remove from the oven and let cool on the cookie sheets for a few minutes, then transfer to wire racks to cool completely. Mix the confectioners' sugar with the water to a thick consistency. Place the frosting in a small plastic bag and cut a tiny hole in one corner. Use the frosting to draw buttons or clothes shapes on the cooled cookies.

party cookies

ingredients

MAKES 16

4 oz/115 g butter, softened,
    plus extra for greasing
4 oz/115 g/generous $^1/_2$ cup
    brown sugar
1 tbsp corn syrup
$^1/_2$ tsp vanilla extract
6 oz/175 g/1$^1/_4$ cups
    self-rising flour
3 oz/85 g sugar-coated
    chocolate beans

method

1 Grease 2 cookie sheets. Place the butter and sugar in a bowl and beat together with an electric whisk until light and fluffy, then beat in the syrup and vanilla extract.

2 Sift in half the flour and work it into the mixture. Stir in the chocolate beans and the remaining flour and work the dough together using a spatular.

3 Roll the dough into 16 balls and place them on the prepared cookie sheets, spaced well apart to allow for spreading. Do not flatten them. Bake in a preheated oven, 350°F/180°C, for 10–12 minutes, or until pale golden at the edges. Remove from the oven and let cool on the cookie sheets for 2 minutes, then transfer to wire racks to cool completely.

simply delicious

This chapter has recipes that are less indulgent, less showy, a little more simple and down-to-earth—but by no means boring!

Weekends are a great time for having a lazy "brunch," that not-quite-breakfast, not-quite-lunch meal that goes hand in hand with reading your favorite magazine and catching up with the latest gossip with your family and friends. For a stylish brunch, make Doughnut Muffins, Lime and Poppy Seed Muffins, and Simple Cinnamon Rolls. The aromas wafting from the oven will be marvelous, and while you are waiting for them to cool a little, you can make a stack of Apple Pancakes to serve with maple syrup butter.

For a simple but delicious accompaniment to your mid-morning cup of coffee, try Gingernuts—home-made are so much better than store-bought, a Drizzled Honey Cupcake, a fruity Rock Drop, or a crumbly Currant Cake. Almond Biscotti are absolutely perfect for dunking in a frothy cappuccino, and also make elegant petits fours to serve with after-dinner coffee.

On a cold winter's afternoon, serve Buttermilk Scones spread with whipped cream and strawberry jelly, Sticky Gingerbread Cupcakes, warm, spicy Griddle Cakes, lemony Queen Cakes, and buttery Shortbread Fans. Very satisfying!

lime & poppy seed muffins

ingredients

MAKES 12

6 fl oz/175 ml/^{3}/$_4$ cup
    sunflower or peanut oil,
    plus extra for oiling
    (if using)
8 oz/225 g/1^1/$_2$ cups
    all-purpose flour
1 tsp baking powder
^{1}/$_2$ tsp salt
8 oz/225 g/scant 1^1/$_4$ cups
    superfine sugar
1 large egg
1 large egg white
5 fl oz/150 ml/^{2}/$_3$ cup milk
1 tbsp lime juice
1 tbsp grated lime rind
2 tsp poppy seeds

to decorate

2 tsp grated lime rind
1–2 tsp poppy seeds

method

1 Oil a 12-cup muffin pan with sunflower oil, or line it with 12 muffin paper liners.

2 Sift the flour, baking powder, and salt into a mixing bowl. Then add the superfine sugar and stir together.

3 In a separate bowl, whisk the egg, egg white, remaining sunflower oil, and milk together, then stir in the lime juice and grated lime rind. Add the egg mixture to the flour mixture, then add the poppy seeds and gently stir together. Do not overstir the batter—it is fine for it to be a little lumpy.

4 Divide the muffin batter evenly among the 12 cups in the muffin pan or the paper liners (they should be about two-thirds full). Sprinkle over grated lime rind and poppy seeds to decorate, then bake in a preheated oven, 375°F/190°C, for 25 minutes, or until risen and golden. Serve the muffins warm, or place them on a cooling rack and let cool.

doughnut muffins

ingredients

MAKES 12

6 oz/175 g butter, softened,
   plus extra for greasing

7 oz/200 g/1 cup
   superfine sugar

2 large eggs, lightly beaten

13oz/375g/generous
   2^1/$_2$ cups all-purpose flour

^{3}/$_4$ tbsp baking powder

^{1}/$_4$ tsp baking soda

pinch of salt

^{1}/$_2$ tsp freshly grated nutmeg

9 fl oz/250 ml/generous
   1 cup milk

topping

3^1/$_2$ oz/100 g/^{1}/$_2$ cup
   superfine sugar

1 tsp ground cinnamon

2 tbsp butter, melted

method

1 Grease a deep 12-cup muffin pan. In a large bowl, beat the butter and sugar together until light and creamy. Add the eggs, a little at a time, beating well between additions.

2 Sift the flour, baking powder, baking soda, salt, and nutmeg together. Add half to the creamed mixture with half of the milk. Gently fold the ingredients together before incorporating the remaining flour and milk. Spoon the mixture into the prepared muffin pan, filling each hole to about two-thirds full. Bake in a preheated oven, 350°F/180°C, for 15–20 minutes, or until the muffins are lightly brown and firm to the touch.

3 For the topping, mix the sugar and cinnamon together. While the muffins are still warm from the oven, brush lightly with melted butter, and sprinkle over the cinnamon and sugar mixture. Eat warm or cold.

sticky gingerbread cupcakes

ingredients

MAKES 16

4 oz/115 g/generous ³/₄ cup
    all-purpose flour
2 tsp ground ginger
³/₄ tsp ground cinnamon
1 piece of preserved
    ginger, minced
³/₄ tsp baking soda
4 tbsp milk
6 tbsp butter, softened,
    or soft margarine
2¹/₂ oz/70 g/generous ¹/₃ cup
    firmly packed brown sugar
2 tbsp molasses
2 eggs, lightly beaten
pieces of preserved ginger,
    to decorate

frosting

6 tbsp butter, softened
6 oz/175 g/1¹/₂ cups
    confectioners' sugar
2 tbsp ginger syrup from the
    preserved ginger jar

method

1 Put 16 paper baking cases in a muffin pan, or place 16 double-layer paper cases on a cookie sheet.

2 Sift the flour, ground ginger, and cinnamon together into a bowl. Add the minced ginger and toss in the flour mixture until well coated. In a separate bowl, dissolve the baking soda in the milk.

3 Put the butter and sugar in a bowl and beat together until fluffy. Beat in the molasses, then gradually add the eggs, beating well after each addition. Beat in the flour mixture, then gradually beat in the milk. Spoon the batter into the paper cases.

4 Bake the cupcakes in a preheated oven, 325°F/160°C, for 20 minutes, or until well risen and golden brown. Transfer to a wire rack and let cool.

5 To make the frosting, put the butter in a bowl and beat until fluffy. Sift in the sugar, add the ginger syrup, and beat together until smooth and creamy. Slice the preserved ginger into thin slivers or chop finely.

6 When the cupcakes are cold, spread the frosting on top of each cupcake, then decorate with pieces of ginger.

drizzled honey cupcakes

ingredients

MAKES 12

3 oz/85 g/generous $^1/_2$ cup
    self-rising white flour
$^1/_4$ tsp ground cinnamon
pinch of ground cloves
pinch of grated nutmeg
6 tbsp butter, softened
3 oz/85 g/scant $^1/_2$ cup
    superfine sugar
1 tbsp honey
finely grated rind of 1 orange
2 eggs, lightly beaten
1$^1/_2$ oz/40 g/$^3/_4$ cup walnut
    pieces, minced

topping

$^1/_2$ oz/15 g/$^1/_8$ cup walnut
    pieces, minced
$^1/_4$ tsp ground cinnamon
2 tbsp honey
juice of 1 orange

method

1 Put 12 paper baking cases in a muffin pan, or place 12 double-layer paper cases on a cookie sheet.

2 Sift the flour, cinnamon, cloves, and nutmeg together into a bowl. Put the butter and sugar in a separate bowl and beat together until light and fluffy. Beat in the honey and orange rind, then gradually add the eggs, beating well after each addition. Using a metal spoon, fold in the flour mixture. Stir in the walnuts, then spoon the batter into the paper cases.

3 Bake the cupcakes in a preheated oven, 375ºF/190ºC, for 20 minutes, or until well risen and golden brown. Transfer to a wire rack and let cool.

4 To make the topping, mix together the walnuts and cinnamon. Put the honey and orange juice in a pan and heat gently, stirring, until combined.

5 When the cupcakes have almost cooled, prick the tops all over with a fork or skewer and then drizzle with the warm honey mixture. Sprinkle the walnut mixture over the top of each cupcake and serve warm or cold.

marbled chocolate cupcakes

ingredients

MAKES 21

6 oz/175 g/³/₄ cup soft
    margarine
6 oz/175 g/generous ³/₄ cup
    superfine sugar
3 eggs
6 oz/175 g/scant 1¹/₄ cups
    self-rising white flour
2 tbsp milk
2 oz/55 g semisweet
    chocolate, melted

method

1 Put 21 paper baking cases in a muffin pan, or place 21 double-layer paper cases on a cookie sheet.

2 Put the margarine, sugar, eggs, flour, and milk in a large bowl and, using an electric hand whisk, beat together until just smooth.

3 Divide the batter between 2 bowls. Add the melted chocolate to one bowl and stir together until well mixed. Using a teaspoon, and alternating the chocolate batter with the plain batter, put four half-teaspoons into each paper case.

4 Bake the cupcakes in a preheated oven, 350°F/180°C, for 20 minutes, or until well risen and springy to the touch. Transfer to a wire rack and let cool.

carrot cake

ingredients

MAKES 6

butter, for greasing

4 oz/115 g/scant 1 cup
   self-rising flour

pinch of salt

1 tsp ground allspice

$^1/_2$ tsp ground nutmeg

6 oz/175 g/$^3/_4$ cup
   soft brown sugar

2 eggs, beaten

5 tbsp sunflower oil

6 oz/175 g/$^3/_4$ cup (packed)
   grated carrots

1 banana, chopped

1oz/25g/$^1/_4$ cup chopped
   toasted mixed nuts

frosting

3 tbsp butter, softened

3 tbsp cream cheese

6 oz/175 g/1$^1/_2$ cups
   confectioners' sugar, sifted

1 tsp orange juice

grated rind of $^1/_2$ orange

walnut halves or pieces,
   to decorate

method

1 Grease a 7-inch/18-cm square cake pan with butter and line with parchment paper. Sift the flour, salt, allspice, and nutmeg into a bowl. Stir in the brown sugar, then stir in the eggs and oil. Add the carrots, banana, and chopped mixed nuts and mix together well.

2 Spoon the mixture into the prepared cake pan and level the surface. Transfer to a preheated oven, 375°F/190°C, and bake for 55 minutes, or until golden and just firm to the touch. Remove from the oven and let cool. When cool enough to handle, turn out on to a wire rack and let cool completely.

3 To make the frosting, put the butter, cream cheese, confectioners' sugar, and orange juice and rind into a bowl and beat together until creamy. Spread the frosting over the top of the cold cake, then use a fork to make shallow wavy lines in the frosting. Scatter over the walnuts, cut the cake into bars, and serve.

simple cinnamon rolls

ingredients

MAKES 8 ROLLS

12 oz/350 g/scant 2$\frac{1}{2}$ cups
   self-rising flour
pinch of salt
2 tbsp superfine sugar
1 tsp ground cinnamon
3$\frac{1}{2}$ oz/100 g butter, melted,
   plus extra for greasing
2 egg yolks
7 fl oz/200 ml/scant 1 cup
   milk, plus extra for glazing

filling

1 tsp ground cinnamon
2 oz/55 g/generous $\frac{1}{4}$ cup
   brown sugar
2 tbsp superfine sugar
1 tbsp butter, melted

frosting

4$\frac{1}{2}$ oz/125 g/generous 1 cup
   confectioners' sugar, sifted
2 tbsp cream cheese, softened
1 tbsp butter, softened
about 2 tbsp boiling water
1 tsp vanilla extract

method

1 Grease an 8-inch/20-cm round pan and line the bottom with parchment paper.

2 Mix the flour, salt, superfine sugar, and cinnamon together in a bowl. Whisk the butter, egg yolks, and milk together and combine with the dry ingredients to make a soft dough. Turn out onto a large piece of waxed paper, lightly sprinkled with flour, and roll out to a rectangle 12 x 10 inches/30 x 25 cm.

3 To make the filling, mix the ingredients together, spread evenly over the dough and roll up, jelly-roll style, to form a log. Using a sharp knife, cut the dough into 8 even-size slices and pack into the prepared pan. Brush gently with extra milk and bake in a preheated oven, 350°F/180°C, for 30–35 minutes, or until golden brown. Remove from the oven and let cool for 5 minutes before removing from the pan.

4 Sift the confectioners' sugar into a large bowl and make a well in the center. Place the cream cheese and butter in the center, pour over the water, and stir to mix. Add extra boiling water, a few drops at a time, until the frosting coats the back of a spoon. Stir in the vanilla extract. Drizzle over the rolls. Serve warm or cold.

buttermilk scones

ingredients

MAKES 8

10^1/$_2$ oz/300 g/generous
   2 cups self-rising flour,
   plus extra for dusting
1 tsp baking powder
pinch of salt
2 oz/55 g cold butter, cut into
   pieces, plus extra
   for greasing
1^1/$_2$ oz/40 g/scant ^{1}/$_4$ cup
   golden superfine sugar
10 fl oz/300 ml/1^1/$_4$ cups
   buttermilk
2 tbsp milk
whipped cream, to serve
strawberry jelly, to serve

method

1 Sift the flour, baking powder, and salt into a bowl. Add the butter and rub in until the mixture resembles fine bread crumbs. Add the sugar and buttermilk and quickly mix together.

2 Turn the mixture out onto a floured counter and knead lightly. Roll out to 1-inch/2.5-cm thick. Using a 2^1/$_2$-inch/6-cm plain or fluted cutter, stamp out biscuits and place on a greased cookie sheet. Gather the trimmings, re-roll, and stamp out more biscuits until all the dough is used up.

3 Brush the tops of the biscuits with milk. Bake in a preheated oven, 425°F/220°C, for 12–15 minutes, or until well risen and golden. Transfer to a wire rack to cool. Split and serve with whipped cream and strawberry jelly.

griddle cakes

ingredients

MAKES 16

8 oz/225 g/generous
    1¹/₂ cups self-rising flour
pinch of salt
2 oz/55 g white cooking fat
2 oz/55 g butter, plus extra
    for greasing
3 oz/85 g/scant ¹/₂ cup
    golden superfine sugar
3 oz/85 g/generous
    ¹/₂ cup currants
1 egg, beaten
1 tbsp milk (optional)
superfine sugar, for dusting

method

1 Sift the flour and salt into a bowl. Add the white cooking fat and butter and rub it in until the mixture resembles bread crumbs. Stir in the sugar and currants. Add the egg and a little milk, if necessary, to make a soft, but not sticky, dough.

2 On a floured counter, roll out the dough to ¹/₄ inch/5 mm thick. Stamp into circles with a 2¹/₂-inch/6-cm plain or fluted cutter. Gather the trimmings, re-roll, and stamp out more biscuits until all the dough is used up.

3 Grease a griddle or heavy-bottom skillet and set over low heat. Cook the biscuits for 3 minutes on each side, or until golden brown. Dust generously with superfine sugar and serve warm or cold.

apple pancakes
with maple syrup butter

ingredients

MAKES 18 PANCAKES
TO SERVE 4–6

7 oz/200 g/scant 1^1/$_2$ cups
   self-rising flour
3^1/$_2$ oz/100 g/^{1}/$_2$ cup
   superfine sugar
1 tsp ground cinnamon
1 egg
7 fl oz/200 ml/scant
   1 cup milk
2 apples, peeled and grated
1 tsp butter

maple syrup butter

3 oz/85 g butter, softened
3 tbsp maple syrup

method

1 Mix the flour, sugar, and cinnamon in a bowl and make a well in the center. Beat the egg and the milk together and pour into the well. Using a wooden spoon, gently incorporate the dry ingredients into the liquid until well combined, then stir in the grated apple.

2 Heat the butter in a large nonstick skillet over low heat until melted and bubbling. Add tablespoons of the pancake mixture to form 3^1/$_2$-inch/9-cm circles. Cook each pancake for about 1 minute, until it starts to bubble lightly on the top and looks set, then flip it over and cook the other side for 30 seconds, or until cooked through. The pancakes should be golden brown; if not, increase the heat a little. Remove from the skillet and keep warm. Repeat the process until all of the pancake batter has been used up (it is not necessary to add extra butter).

3 To make the maple syrup butter, melt the butter with the maple syrup in a pan over low heat and stir until combined. To serve, place the pancakes on serving dishes and spoon over the flavored butter. Serve warm.

queen cakes

ingredients

MAKES 18

8 tbsp butter, softened,
  or soft margarine

4 oz/115 g/generous $^1/_2$ cup
  superfine sugar

2 large eggs, lightly beaten

4 tsp lemon juice

6 oz/175 g/scant $1^1/_4$ cups
  self-rising white flour

4 oz/115 g/$^3/_4$ cup currants

2–4 tbsp milk, if necessary

method

1 Put 18 paper baking cases in a muffin pan, or place 18 double-layer paper cases on a cookie sheet.

2 Put the butter and sugar in a bowl and beat together until light and fluffy. Gradually beat in the eggs, then beat in the lemon juice with 1 tablespoon of the flour. Using a metal spoon, fold in the remaining flour and the currants, adding a little milk if necessary to give a soft dropping consistency. Spoon the batter into the paper cases.

3 Bake the cupcakes in a preheated oven, 375°F/190°C, for 15–20 minutes, or until well risen and golden brown. Transfer to a wire rack and let cool.

rock drops

ingredients

MAKES 8

$3^{1}/_{2}$ oz/100 g butter, cut into
   small pieces, plus extra
   for greasing
7 oz/200 g/$1^{1}/_{2}$ cups
   all-purpose flour
2 tsp baking powder
$2^{3}/_{4}$ oz/75 g/scant $^{1}/_{2}$ cup
   golden superfine sugar
$3^{1}/_{2}$ oz/100 g/$^{1}/_{2}$ cup golden
   raisins
1 oz/25 g/$^{1}/_{4}$ cup candied
   cherries, finely chopped
1 egg, beaten
2 tbsp milk

method

1 Lightly grease a cookie sheet, large enough for 8 big rock drops, with a little butter.

2 Sift the flour and baking powder into a mixing bowl. Rub in the butter with your fingertips until the mixture resembles fine bread crumbs. Stir in the sugar, golden raisins, and chopped candied cherries, mixing well. Add the beaten egg and the milk to the mixture and mix to form a soft dough.

3 Spoon 8 mounds of the mixture onto the prepared cookie sheet, spacing them well apart as they will spread while cooking. Bake in a preheated oven, 400°F/200°C, for 15–20 minutes, until firm to the touch.

4 Remove the rock drops from the cookie sheet. Either serve immediately or transfer to a wire rack and let cool before serving.

currant cakes

ingredients

MAKES 10–12

14 oz/400 g ready-made
   puff pastry
2 tbsp all-purpose flour,
   for dusting
2 oz/55 g butter, softened
2 oz/55 g/generous $^1/_4$ cup
   soft brown sugar
3 oz/85 g/$^1/_2$ cup currants
1 oz /25 g/$^1/_4$ cup
   mixed candied
   citrus peel, chopped
$^1/_2$ tsp ground mixed spice
   (optional)
1 egg white, lightly beaten
1 tsp superfine sugar

method

1 Roll out the pastry thinly, using the flour to dust the counter and the rolling pin. Cut into rounds using a 3$^1/_2$-inch/9-cm cutter. Fold the trimmings carefully, re-roll and repeat the cuttings to give a total of 10–12 rounds.

2 In a bowl, mix together the butter and soft brown sugar until creamy, then add the dried fruit and mixed spice, if using.

3 Put a teaspoon of the filling in the center of each pastry round. Draw the edges of the circles together and pinch the edges over the filling. Reshape each cake into a round. Turn the cakes over and lightly roll them with the rolling pin until the currants just show through. Score with a knife into a lattice pattern. Place on a greased cookie sheet and let rest for 10–15 minutes.

4 Brush the cakes with the egg white, sprinkle with the superfine sugar, and bake at the top of a preheated oven, 425°F/220°C, for about 15 minutes until golden brown and crisp.

5 Transfer to a wire rack and sprinkle with a little more sugar if desired. Serve immediately, or store in an airtight tin for up to a week and reheat before serving.

orange & walnut cakes

ingredients

MAKES ABOUT 18

14 oz/400 g/3 cups
   self-rising flour
$^1/_2$ tsp baking soda
$^1/_2$ tsp ground cinnamon
$^1/_4$ tsp ground cloves
pinch of grated nutmeg
pinch of salt
10 fl oz/300 ml/1$^1/_4$ cups
   olive oil
2$^3/_4$ oz/75 g/$^1/_3$ cup
   superfine sugar
finely grated rind and juice
   of 1 large orange

topping

1 oz/25 g/$^1/_4$ cup walnut
   pieces, chopped finely
$^1/_2$ tsp ground cinnamon

syrup

6 oz/175 g/$^1/_2$ cup
   Greek honey
4 fl oz/125 ml/$^1/_2$ cup water
juice of 1 small lemon
juice of 1 small orange or
   1 tbsp orange flower water

method

1 Sift together the flour, baking soda, cinnamon, cloves, nutmeg, and salt.

2 Put the oil and sugar in a bowl and beat together. Add the orange rind and juice, then gradually beat in the flour mixture. Turn the mixture onto a lightly floured surface and knead for 2–3 minutes, until smooth.

3 Take small, egg-size pieces of dough and shape into ovals. Place on cookie sheets, allowing room for spreading and, with the back of a fork, press the top of each cake twice to make a criss-cross design. Bake the cakes in a preheated oven, 350°F/180°C, for about 20 minutes, until lightly browned. Transfer to a wire rack and let cool.

4 To make the topping, mix together the walnuts and cinnamon. To make the syrup, put the honey and water in a pan, bring to a boil, then let simmer for 5 minutes. Remove from the heat and add the lemon juice and orange juice or orange flower water.

5 When the cakes have almost cooled, using a slotted spoon, submerge each cake in the hot syrup and leave for about 1 minute. Place on a tray and top each with the walnut mixture. Let cool completely before serving.

mincemeat crumble bars

ingredients

MAKES 12

14 oz/400 g/1^1/$_3$ cups ready-
    made mincemeat
confectioners' sugar,
    for dusting

bottom layer

5 oz/140 g butter, plus
    extra for greasing
3 oz/85 g/scant ^{1}/$_2$ cup
    golden superfine sugar
5 oz/150 g/1 cup
    all-purpose flour
3 oz/85 g/scant ^{2}/$_3$ cup
    cornstarch

topping

4 oz/115 g/generous ^{3}/$_4$ cup
    self-rising flour
6 tbsp butter, cut into pieces
3 oz/85 g/scant ^{1}/$_2$ cup
    golden superfine sugar
1 oz/25 g/^{1}/$_4$ cup slivered
    almonds

method

1 Grease a shallow 11 x 8-inch/28 x 20-cm cake pan. To make the bottom layer, beat the butter and sugar together in a bowl until light and fluffy. Sift in the flour and cornstarch and, with your hands, bring the mixture together to form a ball. Push the dough into the cake pan, pressing it out and into the corners, then let chill in the refrigerator for 20 minutes. Bake in a preheated oven, 400°F/ 200°C, for 12–15 minutes, or until puffed and golden.

2 To make the crumble topping, place the flour, butter, and sugar in a bowl and rub together into coarse crumbs. Stir in the slivered almonds.

3 Spread the mincemeat over the bottom layer and scatter the crumbs on top. Bake in the oven for an additional 20 minutes, or until golden brown. Let cool slightly, then cut into 12 pieces and let cool completely. Dust with sifted confectioners' sugar, then serve.

shortbread fans

ingredients

MAKES 8 PIECES

6 oz/175 g/scant $1^1/4$ cups
   all-purpose flour, plus
   1 tbsp for dusting

pinch of salt

2 oz /55 g/generous $^1/4$ cup
   superfine sugar

4 oz/115 g butter, cut into
   small pieces, plus extra
   for greasing

2 tsp golden superfine sugar

method

1 Mix together the flour, salt, and sugar. Rub the butter into the dry ingredients. Continue to work the mixture until it forms a soft dough. Make sure you do not overwork the dough or the shortbread will be tough, not crumbly as it should be.

2 Lightly press the dough into a greased 20-cm/8-inch fluted cake pan. Alternatively, roll out the dough on a lightly floured counter, place on a cookie sheet, and pinch the edges to form a scalloped pattern.

3 Mark into 8 pieces with a knife. Prick the shortbread all over with a fork and bake in the center of a preheated oven, 150°C/300°F, for 45–50 minutes until the shortbread is firm and just colored.

4 Let cool in the tin and dredge with the sugar. Cut into portions and remove to a wire rack. Store in an airtight container in a cool place until needed.

almond biscotti

ingredients

MAKES 20–24

9 oz/250 g/1^3/$_4$ cups
   all-purpose flour,
   plus extra for dusting
1 tsp baking powder
pinch of salt
5^1/$_2$ oz/150 g/^{3}/$_4$ cup golden
   superfine sugar
2 eggs, beaten
finely grated rind of
   1 unwaxed orange
3^1/$_2$ oz/100 g/^{2}/$_3$ cup whole
   blanched almonds,
   lightly toasted

method

1 Sift the flour, baking powder, and salt into a bowl. Add the sugar, eggs, and orange rind and mix to a dough, then knead in the almonds.

2 Using your hands, roll the dough into a ball, cut in half, and roll each portion into a log about 1^1/$_2$ inches/4 cm in diameter. Place on a cookie sheet lightly dusted with flour and bake in a preheated oven, 350°F/180°C, for 10 minutes. Remove from the oven and let cool for 5 minutes.

3 Using a serrated knife, cut the logs into ^{1}/$_2$-inch/1-cm thick diagonal slices. Arrange the slices on the cookie sheet and return to the oven for 15 minutes, or until slightly golden. Transfer to a wire rack to cool and crispen.

lavender cookies

ingredients

MAKES 12

2 oz/55 g/¹/₄ cup golden
   superfine sugar, plus
   extra for dusting
1 tsp chopped lavender leaves
4 oz/115 g butter, softened,
   plus extra for greasing
finely grated rind of 1 lemon
6 oz/175 g/1¹/₄ cups
   all-purpose flour

method

1 Place the sugar and lavender leaves in a food processor. Process until the lavender is very finely chopped, then add the butter and lemon rind and process until light and fluffy. Transfer to a large bowl. Sift in the flour and beat until the mixture forms a stiff dough.

2 Place the dough on a sheet of parchment paper and place another sheet on top. Gently press down with a rolling pin and roll out to ¹/₈–¹/₄-inch/3–5-mm thick. Remove the top sheet of paper and stamp out circles from the dough using a 2³/₄-inch/7-cm round cookie cutter. Re-knead and re-roll the dough trimmings and stamp out more cookies.

3 Using a spatula, carefully transfer the cookies to a large, greased cookie sheet. Prick the cookies with a fork and bake in a preheated oven, 300°F/150°C, for 12 minutes, or until pale golden brown. Let cool on the cookie sheet for 2 minutes, then transfer to a wire rack to cool completely.

gingernuts

ingredients

MAKES 30

12 oz/350 g/3 cups
  self-rising flour

pinch of salt

7 oz/200 g/1 cup
  superfine sugar

1 tbsp ground ginger

1 tsp baking soda

4½ oz/125 g butter,
  plus extra for greasing

2¾ oz/75 g/¼ cups
  corn syrup

1 egg, beaten

1 tsp grated orange zest

method

1 Sift the self-rising flour, salt, sugar, ginger, and baking soda into a large mixing bowl.

2 Melt the butter and corn syrup together in a pan over a low heat. Remove the pan from the heat and let the butter and syrup mixture cool slightly, then pour it onto the dry ingredients. Add the egg and orange zest and mix thoroughly to form a dough.

3 Using your hands, carefully shape the dough into 30 even-size balls. Place the balls well apart on several cookie sheets lightly greased with butter, then flatten them slightly with your fingers.

4 Bake in a preheated oven, 325°F/160°C, for 15–20 minutes, until golden. Carefully transfer the cookies to a wire rack to cool.

orange cream cheese cookies

ingredients

MAKES 30

8 oz/225 g butter,
  plus extra for greasing
7 oz/200 g/1 cup
  packed brown sugar
3 oz/85 g/scant $^1/_2$ cup
  cream cheese
1 egg, lightly beaten
12 oz/350 g/generous
  $2^1/_3$ cups all-purpose flour
1 tsp baking soda
1 tbsp fresh orange juice
1 tsp finely grated orange rind,
  plus extra for decorating
raw brown sugar,
  for sprinkling

method

1 Put the butter, sugar, and cream cheese in a large bowl and beat until light and fluffy. Beat in the egg. Sift in the flour and baking soda and add the orange juice and rind. Mix well.

2 Drop about 30 rounded tablespoonfuls of the batter onto a large, greased cookie sheet, making sure that they are well spaced apart. Sprinkle with the raw brown sugar.

3 Bake in a preheated oven, 375°F/190°C, for 10 minutes, or until the cookies are light golden brown at the edges.

4 Let cool on a wire rack. Decorate with orange rind before serving.

healthy
options

Leading a healthy lifestyle is sensible, desirable, and in some cases an absolute necessity—and it always seems to suggest an element of deprivation when it comes to those edible treats that add so much pleasure to life. If you have been diagnosed with diabetes or a heart problem, or have an intolerance to gluten or lactose, you will be pleased to know that you can still have the occasional cake.

If you are on a lowfat eating plan, the muffin recipes are ideal for you. Try Banana and Date Muffins, or Cranberry or Blueberry—and, to look at them, you won't believe that Spiced Wholemeal Muffins, Spiced Carrot Cake Muffins, and Chocolate Brownies are also fine for you to eat! Diabetics can enjoy Honey and Lemon Muffins and Sugarless Chocolate Muffins—again, you'll be delighted to discover that these are a delicious option for you.

For a gluten or dairy intolerance, try Banana Muffins with Cinnamon Frosting and Chocolate Orange Mousse Cake—both these recipes use a gluten-free alternative to wheat and a dairy-free margarine.

If you simply want a healthy treat to keep you going through the day, try High-energy Muffins—the slow-release energy in oats will sustain you for hours!

banana muffins with cinnamon frosting

ingredients

MAKES 12

5¹/₂ oz/150 g/generous
   1 cup gluten-free
   all-purpose flour
1 tsp gluten-free baking powder
pinch of salt
5¹/₂ oz/150 g/generous
   ³/4 cup superfine sugar
6 tbsp dairy-free milk
2 eggs, lightly beaten
5¹/₂ oz/150 g dairy-free
   margarine, melted
2 small bananas, mashed

frosting

1³/4 oz/50 g/scant ¹/4 cup
   vegan cream cheese
2 tbsp dairy-free margarine
¹/4 tsp ground cinnamon
3¹/4 oz/90 g/scant 1 cup
   confectioners' sugar

method

1 Place 12 large paper cases in a deep muffin pan. Sift the flour, baking powder, and salt together into a mixing bowl. Stir in the sugar.

2 Whisk the milk, eggs, and margarine together in a separate bowl until combined. Slowly stir into the flour mixture without beating. Fold in the mashed bananas.

3 Spoon the mixture into the paper cases and bake in a preheated oven, 400°F/200°C, for 20 minutes until risen and golden. Turn out onto a wire rack and let cool.

4 To make the frosting, beat the cream cheese and margarine together in a bowl, then beat in the cinnamon and confectioners' sugar until smooth and creamy. Chill the frosting in the refrigerator for about 15 minutes to firm up, then top each muffin with a spoonful.

banana & date muffins

ingredients

MAKES 12

vegetable oil cooking spray,
	for oiling (if using)

8 oz/225 g/1$\frac{1}{2}$ cups
	all-purpose flour

2 tsp baking powder

$\frac{1}{4}$ tsp salt

$\frac{1}{2}$ tsp allspice

5 tbsp superfine sugar

2 large egg whites

2 ripe bananas, sliced

2 oz/55 g/scant $\frac{1}{2}$ cup
	no-soak dried dates, pitted
	and chopped

4 tbsp skim milk

5 tbsp maple syrup

method

1 Spray a 12-cup muffin pan with vegetable oil cooking spray, or line it with 12 muffin paper liners. Sift the flour, baking powder, salt, and allspice into a mixing bowl. Add the superfine sugar and mix together.

2 In a separate bowl, whisk the egg whites together. Mash the sliced bananas in a separate bowl, then add them to the egg whites. Add the dates, then pour in the skim milk and maple syrup and stir together gently to mix. Add the banana and date mixture to the flour mixture and then gently stir together until just combined. Do not overstir the batter—it is fine for it to be a little lumpy.

3 Divide the muffin batter evenly among the 12 cups in the muffin pan or the paper liners (they should be about two-thirds full). Bake in a preheated oven, 400°F/200°C, for 25 minutes, or until risen and golden. Remove the muffins from the oven and serve warm, or place them on a cooling rack and let cool.

apple & raspberry muffins

ingredients

MAKES 12

3 large baking apples, peeled and cored

16 fl oz/450 ml/generous 1¹/2 cups water

1¹/2 tsp allspice

vegetable oil cooking spray, for oiling (if using)

10¹/2 oz/300 g/generous 2 cups all-purpose whole-wheat flour

1 tbsp baking powder

¹/4 tsp salt

3 tbsp superfine sugar

3 oz/85 g/generous 1 cup fresh raspberries

method

1 Thinly slice 2 baking apples and place them in a pan with 6 tablespoons of the water. Bring to a boil, then reduce the heat. Stir in ¹/2 teaspoon of the allspice, cover the pan, and let simmer, stirring occasionally, for 15–20 minutes until the water has been absorbed. Remove from the heat and let cool. Blend in a food processor until smooth. Stir in the remaining water and mix well.

2 Spray a 12-cup muffin pan with vegetable oil cooking spray, or line it with 12 muffin paper liners. Sift the flour, baking powder, salt, and remaining allspice into a mixing bowl. Then stir in the sugar.

3 Chop the remaining apple and add to the flour mixture. Add the raspberries, then combine gently with the flour mixture until lightly coated. Finally, gently stir in the cooled apple/water mixture. Do not overstir the batter—it is fine for it to be a little lumpy.

4 Divide the muffin batter evenly among the 12 cups in the muffin pan or the paper liners (they should be about two-thirds full). Bake in a preheated oven, 400°F/200°C, for 25 minutes, or until risen and golden. Remove the muffins from the oven and serve warm, or place them on a cooling rack and let cool.

dairy-free berry muffins

ingredients

MAKES 12

1 large baking apple, peeled, cored, and thinly sliced

3 tbsp water

1 tsp allspice

2 tbsp sunflower or peanut oil, plus extra for oiling (if using)

8 oz/225 g/1¹/₂ cups all-purpose white or whole-wheat flour

1 tbsp baking powder

¹/₄ tsp salt

1¹/₂ oz/40 g/scant ¹/₂ cup wheat germ

1 oz/25 g/¹/₄ cup fresh raspberries

1 oz/25 g/¹/₄ cup fresh strawberries, hulled and chopped

6 tbsp maple syrup

6 fl oz/175 ml/³/₄ cup apple juice

method

1 Place the sliced apple and the water in a pan and bring to a boil. Reduce the heat and stir in half of the allspice, then cover the pan and let simmer, stirring occasionally, for 15–20 minutes, or until the water has been absorbed. Remove the pan from the heat and let cool. Transfer the apple mixture to a food processor and blend until smooth.

2 Lightly oil a 12-cup muffin pan with a little sunflower oil, or line the pan with 12 muffin paper liners.

3 Sift the flour, baking powder, salt, and the remaining allspice into a mixing bowl, then stir in the wheat germ.

4 In a separate bowl, mix the raspberries, chopped strawberries, maple syrup, remaining oil, puréed apple, and apple juice together. Add the fruit mixture to the flour mixture and gently stir together until just combined. Do not overstir the batter—it is fine for it to be a little lumpy.

5 Divide the muffin batter evenly among the 12 cups in the muffin pan or the paper liners (they should be about two-thirds full). Transfer to a preheated oven, 375°F/190°C, and bake for 25 minutes, or until risen and golden. Remove from the oven and serve warm, or place them on a cooling rack and let cool.

cranberry muffins

ingredients

MAKES 10

6 oz/175 g/scant 1¹/4 cups
self-rising white flour

2 oz/55 g/scant ¹/2 cup self-
rising whole-wheat flour

1 tsp ground cinnamon

¹/2 tsp baking soda

1 egg, beaten

2¹/2 oz/70 g/scant ¹/4 cup
thin-cut orange
marmalade

5 fl oz/150 ml/²/3 cup
1 or 2 percent milk

5 tbsp corn oil

4 oz/115 g peeled, cored, and
finely diced eating apple

4 oz/115 g/²/3 cup fresh or
frozen cranberries,
thawed if frozen

1 tbsp rolled oats

freshly squeezed orange
juice, to serve

method

1 Line a muffin pan with 10 muffin paper cases.

2 Put the two flours, cinnamon, and baking soda into a mixing bowl and combine thoroughly.

3 Make a well in the center of the flour mixture. In a separate bowl, blend the egg with the marmalade until well combined. Beat the milk and oil into the egg mixture, then pour into the dry ingredients, stirring lightly. Do not overmix—the batter should be slightly lumpy. Quickly stir in the apple and cranberries.

4 Spoon the batter evenly into the paper cases and sprinkle the oats over each muffin. Bake in a preheated oven, 400°F/200°C, for 20–25 minutes, or until well risen and golden, and a skewer inserted into the center of a muffin comes out clean.

5 Lift out the muffins and transfer onto a wire rack. Let stand for 5–10 minutes, or until slightly cooled. Peel off the paper cases and serve warm with glasses of freshly squeezed orange juice. These muffins are best eaten on the day they are made—any leftover muffins should be stored in an airtight container and consumed within 24 hours.

blueberry muffins

ingredients

MAKES 12

vegetable oil cooking spray,
    for oiling (if using)
8 oz/225 g/generous
    1½ cups all-purpose flour
1 tsp baking soda
¼ tsp salt
1 tsp allspice
4 oz/115 g/generous ½ cup
    superfine sugar
3 large egg whites
3 tbsp lowfat margarine
5 fl oz/150 ml/⅔ cup
    thick lowfat plain or
    blueberry-flavored yogurt
1 tsp vanilla extract
3 oz/85 g/¾ cup
    fresh blueberries

method

1 Spray a 12-cup muffin pan with vegetable oil cooking spray, or line it with 12 muffin paper liners.

2 Sift the flour, baking soda, salt, and half of the allspice into a large mixing bowl. Add 6 tablespoons of the superfine sugar and mix together.

3 In a separate bowl, whisk the egg whites together. Add the margarine, yogurt, and vanilla extract and mix together well, then stir in the fresh blueberries until thoroughly mixed. Add the fruit mixture to the flour mixture, then gently stir together until just combined. Do not overstir the batter—it is fine for it to be a little lumpy.

4 Divide the muffin batter evenly among the 12 cups in the muffin pan or the paper liners (they should be about two-thirds full). Mix the remaining sugar with the remaining allspice, then sprinkle the mixture over the muffins. Transfer to a preheated oven, 375°F/190°C, and bake for 25 minutes, or until risen and golden. Remove the muffins from the oven and serve warm, or place them on a cooling rack and let cool.

fruity muffins

ingredients

MAKES 10

10 oz/275 g/2 cups
   self-rising whole-
   wheat flour

2 tsp baking powder

2 tbsp brown sugar

3 oz/85 g/generous $^1/_2$ cup
   no-soak dried apricots,
   finely chopped

1 banana, mashed with
   1 tbsp orange juice

1 tsp finely grated
   orange rind

10 fl oz/300 ml/1$^1/_4$ cups
   skim milk

1 large egg, beaten

3 tbsp sunflower or peanut oil

2 tbsp rolled oats

fruit spread, honey, or maple
   syrup, to serve

method

1 Line 10 cups of a 12-cup muffin pan with muffin paper liners. Sift the flour and baking powder into a mixing bowl, adding any husks that remain in the strainer. Stir in the sugar and chopped apricots.

2 Make a well in the center and add the mashed banana, orange rind, milk, beaten egg, and oil. Mix together well to form a thick batter and divide the mixture evenly among the muffin liners.

3 Sprinkle with a few rolled oats and bake in a preheated oven, 400°F/200°C, for 25–30 minutes until well risen and firm to the touch, or until a toothpick inserted into the center comes out clean.

4 Remove the muffins from the oven and place them on a cooling rack to cool slightly. Serve the muffins while still warm with a little fruit spread, honey, or maple syrup.

honey & lemon muffins

ingredients

MAKES 12

1³/₄ oz/50 g/¹/₄ cup
   unrefined superfine sugar
2 tbsp unsalted butter, melted
   and cooled slightly
5 fl oz/150 ml/²/₃ cup
   buttermilk
2 eggs, beaten
4 tbsp flower honey
finely grated rind of 1 lemon
   and juice of ¹/₂ lemon
8 oz/225 g/generous 1¹/₂ cups
   all-purpose flour
5¹/₂ oz/150 g/2³/₄ cups
   oat bran
1¹/₂ tbsp baking powder

method

1 Line a 12-hole muffin pan with muffin paper liners. Put the sugar into a pitcher and add the butter, buttermilk, eggs, half the honey, and lemon rind. Mix briefly to combine.

2 Sift the flour into a large mixing bowl, add the oat bran and baking powder, and stir to combine. Make a well in the center of the flour mixture and add the buttermilk mixture. Quickly mix together—do not overmix; the batter should be slightly lumpy.

3 Spoon the batter into the paper cases and bake in a preheated oven, 350°F/180°C, for 25 minutes. Turn out onto a wire rack.

4 Mix the lemon juice with the remaining honey in a small bowl or pitcher and drizzle over the muffins while they are still hot. Let the muffins stand for 10 minutes before serving.

spiced carrot cake muffins

ingredients

MAKES 12

2 tbsp sunflower or peanut
   oil, plus extra for oiling
   (if using)
scant $3/4$ cup all-purpose
   white flour
$3^1/2$ oz/100 g/$3/4$ cup all-
   purpose whole-wheat flour
1 tsp baking soda
$1/4$ tsp salt
1 tsp ground cinnamon
$1/2$ tsp ground ginger
2 tbsp superfine sugar
2 large egg whites
5 tbsp skim or lowfat milk
8 oz/225 g canned pineapple
   chunks in juice, drained,
   chopped, and mashed
9 oz/250 g carrots, grated
$1^1/2$ oz/40 g/$1/4$ cup
   golden raisins
$1^1/2$ oz/40 g/scant $1/2$ cup
   shelled walnuts, chopped

topping

8 oz/225 g/$1^1/8$ cups Quark
   (or any lowfat soft cheese)
$1^1/3$ tbsp superfine sugar
$1^1/2$ tsp vanilla extract
$1^1/2$ tsp ground cinnamon

method

1 Oil a 12-cup muffin pan with sunflower oil, or line it with 12 muffin paper liners. Sift both flours, baking soda, salt, cinnamon, and ginger into a mixing bowl. Add the superfine sugar and mix together.

2 In a separate bowl, whisk the egg whites together, then mix in the milk and remaining oil. Add the mashed pineapple, the carrots, golden raisins, and walnuts and stir together gently. Add the fruit mixture to the flour mixture and gently stir until just combined. Do not overstir the batter—it is fine for it to be a little lumpy.

3 Divide the muffin batter evenly among the 12 cups in the muffin pan or the paper liners (they should be about two-thirds full). Transfer to a preheated oven, 375°F/190°C, and bake for 25 minutes, or until risen and golden, then let cool on a wire rack.

4 While the muffins are in the oven, make the topping. Place the Quark in a mixing bowl with the superfine sugar, vanilla extract, and 1 teaspoon of the cinnamon. Mix together well, then cover with plastic wrap and transfer to the refrigerator until ready to use.

5 When the muffins have cooled to room temperature, remove the topping from the refrigerator and spread some evenly over the top of each muffin. Lightly sprinkle over the remaining cinnamon and serve.

potato & raisin muffins

ingredients

MAKES 12

butter, for greasing and
    serving (optional)
6 oz/175 g mealy
    potatoes, diced
4$\frac{1}{2}$ oz/125 g/scant 1 cup
    self-rising flour, plus
    extra for dusting
2 tbsp brown sugar
1 tsp baking powder
6 oz/175 g/scant
    1 cup raisins
4 large eggs, separated

method

1 Lightly grease and flour a 12-cup muffin
pan. Cook the diced potatoes in a pan of
boiling water for 10 minutes, or until tender.
Drain well and mash until smooth. Transfer
to a mixing bowl and add the flour, sugar,
baking powder, raisins, and egg yolks. Stir well
to mix thoroughly.

2 In a clean, greasefree bowl, whisk the egg
whites until they are standing in peaks. Using
a metal spoon, gently fold them into the potato
mixture until fully incorporated.

3 Divide the batter evenly among the 12 cups
in the muffin pan. Bake the muffins in a
preheated oven, 400°F/200°C, for 10 minutes.
Reduce the oven temperature to 325°F/160°C
and bake the muffins for an additional 7–10
minutes, or until risen.

4 Remove the muffins from the oven and
serve warm, buttered, if you like.

high-energy muffins

ingredients

MAKES 12

5 tbsp sunflower or peanut
   oil, plus extra for oiling
   (if using)
3 oz/85 g/generous $^1/_2$ cup
   whole-wheat flour
$1^3/_4$ oz/50 g/$^1/_2$ cup quick-
   cooking oats
$1^1/_2$ oz/40 g/scant $^1/_2$ cup
   wheat germ
2 tsp baking powder
1 tsp ground cinnamon
$^1/_4$ tsp salt
$1^1/_2$ oz/40 g/$^1/_3$ cup
   no-soak dried dates,
   pitted and chopped
2 oz/55 g/$^1/_3$ cup
   golden raisins
4 oz/115 g/$3^1/_2$ cups
   bran flakes
7 fl oz/200 ml/scant
   1 cup milk
2 large eggs, beaten
5 tbsp honey
4 tbsp corn syrup
4 tbsp molasses

method

1 Oil a 12-cup muffin pan with sunflower oil, or line it with 12 muffin paper liners. Place the flour, oats, wheat germ, baking powder, cinnamon, and salt in a mixing bowl and mix together.

2 In a separate bowl, mix the dates, golden raisins, and bran flakes together. Pour in the milk and stir together. Then stir in the beaten eggs, honey, corn syrup, molasses, and remaining oil. Add the fruit mixture to the flour mixture and then gently stir together until just combined. Do not overstir the batter—it is fine for it to be a little lumpy.

3 Divide the muffin batter evenly among the 12 cups in the muffin pan or the paper liners (they should be about two-thirds full). Transfer to a preheated oven, 375°F/190°C, and bake for 20–25 minutes until risen and golden. Remove the muffins from the oven and serve warm, or place them on a cooling rack and let cool.

spiced whole-wheat muffins

ingredients

SERVES 6

canola or vegetable oil spray
$4^1/_2$ oz/125 g/scant 1 cup
   all-purpose flour
$^1/_2$ tsp baking powder
2 oz/55 g/scant $^1/_2$ cup
   whole-wheat flour
$^1/_2$ tsp ground allspice
1 tbsp canola or vegetable oil
1 egg, lightly beaten
5 fl oz/150 ml/$^2/_3$ cup
   buttermilk
1 tsp grated orange zest
1 tbsp freshly squeezed
   orange juice
1 tsp low-sugar marmalade,
   for glazing

filling

$3^1/_2$ oz/100 g/generous
   $^1/_3$ cup 0% fat strained
   plain yogurt
tsp low-sugar marmalade
tsp grated orange zest
oz/100 g/scant $^1/_2$ cup
   fresh raspberries

method

1 Spray a 6-hole muffin pan lightly with oil.

2 Sift the all-purpose flour with the baking powder into a large mixing bowl. Using a fork, stir in the whole-wheat flour and allspice until thoroughly mixed. Pour in the oil and rub into the flour mixture with your fingertips.

3 In a separate bowl, mix the egg, buttermilk, and orange zest and juice together, then pour into the center of the flour mixture and mix with a metal spoon, being careful not to overmix—the batter should look a little uneven and lumpy.

4 Spoon the batter into the prepared pan to come about three-quarters of the way up the sides of each hole. Bake in a preheated oven, 325°F/160°C, for 30 minutes, or until golden brown and a skewer inserted into the center of a muffin comes out clean. Remove from the oven and transfer to a wire rack. Brush with the marmalade and let cool.

5 For the filling, mix the yogurt with the marmalade and orange zest. Cut the warm muffins through the center and fill with the yogurt mixture and raspberries.

sugarless chocolate muffins

ingredients

MAKES 12

4 tbsp sunflower or peanut
   oil, plus extra for oiling
   (if using)
8 oz/225 g/generous 1½ cups
   all-purpose flour
1 tbsp baking powder
1 tbsp unsweetened cocoa
½ tsp allspice
2 large eggs
6 fl oz/175 ml/¾ cup
   unsweetened orange juice
1 tsp grated orange rind
1½ oz/40 g/generous ½ cup
   fresh blueberries

method

1 Oil a 12-cup muffin pan with sunflower oil, or line it with 12 muffin paper liners. Sift the flour, baking powder, cocoa, and allspice into a large mixing bowl.

2 In a separate bowl, whisk the eggs and the remaining sunflower oil together. Pour in the orange juice, add the grated orange rind and the blueberries, and stir together gently to mix. Add the egg and fruit mixture to the flour mixture and then gently stir together until just combined. Do not overstir the batter—it is fine for it to be a little lumpy.

3 Divide the muffin batter evenly among the 12 cups in the muffin pan or the paper liners (they should be about two-thirds full). Transfer to a preheated oven, 400°F/200°C, and bake for 20 minutes, or until risen and golden. Serve the muffins warm, or place them on a cooling rack and let cool.

carrot bars

ingredients

MAKES 14–16

corn oil, for oiling

6 oz/175 g unsalted butter

3 oz/85 g/scant $^1/_2$ cup
    packed brown sugar

2 eggs, beaten

2 oz/55 g/scant $^1/_2$ cup
    self-rising whole-wheat
    flour, sifted

1 tsp baking powder, sifted

1 tsp ground cinnamon, sifted

4 oz/115 g/$1^1/_4$ cups
    ground almonds

4 oz/115 g carrot,
    coarsely grated

3 oz/85 g/$^1/_2$ cup
    golden raisins

3 oz/85 g/$^1/_2$ cup
    no-soak dried apricots,
    finely chopped

2 oz/55 g/$^3/_8$ cup toasted
    chopped hazelnuts

1 tbsp slivered almonds

method

1 Lightly oil and line a 10 x 8-inch/25 x 20-cm shallow, rectangular baking pan with nonstick parchment paper.

2 Cream the butter and sugar together in a bowl until light and fluffy, then gradually beat in the eggs, adding a little flour after each addition.

3 Add all the remaining ingredients, except the slivered almonds. Spoon the mixture into the prepared pan and smooth the top. Sprinkle with the slivered almonds.

4 Bake in a preheated oven, 350°F/180°C, for 35–45 minutes, or until the mixture is cooked and a skewer inserted into the center comes out clean.

5 Remove from the oven and let cool in the pan. Remove from the pan, discard the lining paper, and cut into bars.

fruit & nut squares

ingredients

MAKES 9

4 oz/115 g unsalted butter, plus extra for greasing

2 tbsp honey

1 egg, beaten

3 oz/85 g/generous ³/₄ cup ground almonds

4 oz/115 g/scant 1 cup no-soak dried apricots, finely chopped

2 oz/55 g/¹/₃ cup dried cherries

2 oz/55 g/generous ¹/₄ cup toasted chopped hazelnuts

1 oz/25 g/¹/₈ cup sesame seeds

3 oz/85 g/scant 1 cup rolled oats

method

1 Lightly grease a 7-inch/18-cm shallow, square baking pan with butter. Beat the remaining butter with the honey in a bowl until creamy, then beat in the egg with the almonds.

2 Add the remaining ingredients and mix together. Press into the prepared pan, ensuring that the mixture is firmly packed. Smooth the top.

3 Bake in a preheated oven, 350°F/180°C, for 20–25 minutes, or until firm to the touch and golden brown.

4 Remove from the oven and let stand for 10 minutes before marking into squares. Let stand until cold before removing from the pan. Store in an airtight container.

super mocha brownies

ingredients

MAKES 12

5$\frac{1}{2}$ oz/150 g good-quality
    semisweet chocolate
    (70 percent cocoa solids)
3$\frac{1}{2}$ oz/100 g dairy-free
    margarine, plus extra
    for greasing
1 tsp strong instant coffee
1 tsp vanilla extract
3$\frac{1}{2}$ oz/100 g/1 cup
    ground almonds
6 oz/175 g/scant 1 cup
    superfine sugar
4 eggs, separated
confectioners' sugar,
    to decorate (optional)

method

1 Grease an 8-inch/20-cm square cake pan and line the bottom.

2 Melt the chocolate and margarine in a heatproof bowl placed over a pan of gently simmering water, making sure that the bottom of the bowl does not touch the water. Stir very occasionally until the chocolate and margarine have melted and are smooth.

3 Carefully remove the bowl from the heat. Let cool slightly, then stir in the coffee and vanilla extract. Add the almonds and sugar and mix well until combined. Lightly beat the egg yolks in a separate bowl, then stir into the chocolate mixture.

4 Whisk the egg whites in a large bowl until they form stiff peaks. Gently fold a large spoonful of the egg whites into the chocolate mixture, then fold in the remainder until completely incorporated.

5 Spoon the mixture into the prepared pan and bake in a preheated oven, 350°F/180°C, for 35–40 minutes, or until risen and firm on top but still slightly gooey in the center. Let cool in the pan, then turn out, remove the lining paper, and cut into 12 pieces. Dust with confectioners' sugar before serving, if liked.

chocolate brownies

ingredients

MAKES 12

butter, for greasing

2 oz/55 g/^{1}/3 cup
   unsweetened pitted dates,
   chopped

2 oz/55 g/^{1}/3 cup no-soak
   dried prunes, chopped

6 tbsp unsweetened
   apple juice

4 eggs, beaten

10^1/2 oz/300 g/1^1/2 cups
   packed brown sugar

1 tsp vanilla extract

4 tbsp lowfat drinking
   chocolate powder, plus
   extra for dusting

2 tbsp unsweetened cocoa

6 oz/175 g/1^1/4 cups
   all-purpose flour

2 oz/55 g/^{1}/3 cup semisweet
   chocolate chips

frosting

4^1/2 oz/125 g/1^1/8 cups
   confectioners' sugar

1–2 tsp water

1 tsp vanilla extract

method

1 Grease and line a 7 x 11-inch/18 x 28-cm cake pan with parchment paper. Place the dates and prunes in a small pan and add the apple juice. Bring to a boil, cover, and let simmer for 10 minutes until soft. Beat to form a smooth paste, then let cool.

2 Place the cooled fruit in a mixing bowl and stir in the eggs, sugar, and vanilla extract. Sift in 4 tablespoons of drinking chocolate, the cocoa, and the flour, and fold in along with the chocolate chips until well incorporated.

3 Spoon the batter into the prepared pan and smooth over the top. Bake in a preheated oven, 350°F/180°C, for 25–30 minutes until firm to the touch or until a skewer inserted into the center comes out clean. Cut into 12 bars and let cool in the pan for 10 minutes. Transfer to a wire rack to cool completely.

4 To make the frosting, sift the sugar into a bowl and mix with enough water and the vanilla extract to form a soft, but not too runny, frosting. Drizzle the frosting over the chocolate brownies and let set. Dust with the extra chocolate powder before serving.

chocolate orange mousse cake

ingredients

SERVES 8

3¹/₂ oz/100 g/¹/₂ cup superfine sugar

3¹/₂ oz/100 g dairy-free margarine, plus extra for greasing

2 eggs, lightly beaten

3¹/₂ oz/100 g³/₄ cup gluten-free all-purpose flour

1 tsp gluten-free baking powder

2 tbsp unsweetened cocoa

finely pared strips of orange rind, to decorate

mousse

7 oz/200 g good-quality semisweet chocolate (about 70 percent cocoa solids)

grated rind of 2 oranges and juice of 1

4 eggs, separated

method

1 Cream the sugar and margarine together in a mixing bowl until pale and fluffy. Gradually add the eggs, beating well with a wooden spoon between each addition. Sift the flour, baking powder, and unsweetened cocoa together, fold half into the egg mixture, then fold in the remainder. Spoon the mixture into a greased and base-lined 9-inch/23-cm round, loose-bottom cake pan and level the surface with the back of a spoon. Bake in a preheated oven, 350°F/180°C, for 20 minutes until risen and firm to the touch. Let cool in the pan.

2 Meanwhile, melt the chocolate in a bowl placed over a pan of gently simmering water, making sure that the bottom of the bowl does not touch the water. Let cool, then stir in the orange rind and juice and the egg yolks.

3 Whisk the egg whites in a large bowl until they form stiff peaks. Gently fold a large spoonful of the egg whites into the chocolate mixture, then fold in the remainder. Spoon the mixture on top of the cooked, cooled sponge and level the top with the back of a spoon. Place in the refrigerator to set. Remove the sides of the pan if not already removed (though not the bottom) before decorating with the orange rind strips and serving.